# TRIPLE
# RIDGE
# FARM

FENSKE FARMLAND

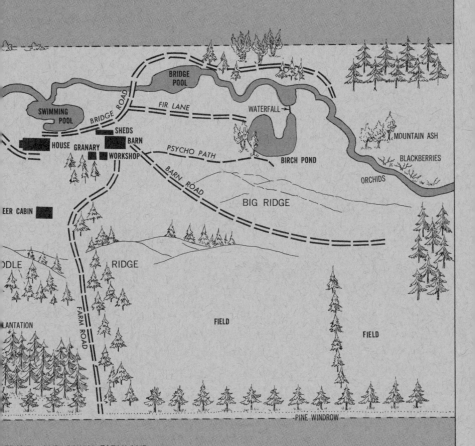

BRIDGE
POOL

SWIMMING
POOL

BRIDGE ROAD

FIR LANE

WATERFALL →

SHEDS

HOUSE GRANARY BARN

WORKSHOP

PSYCHO PATH

MOUNTAIN ASH

BLACKBERRIES

BIRCH POND

ORCHIDS

BARN ROAD

BIG RIDGE

EER CABIN

ODLE

RIDGE

LANTATION

FARM ROAD

FIELD

FIELD

PINE WINDROW

FRAVEL AND SAWIN FARMLAND

# Triple Ridge Farm

# Triple Ridge Farm

## ～ by Ruth Fouts Pochmann ～

*Illustrations by Lydia Rosier*

*William Morrow & Company, Inc.*

NEW YORK 1968

Published simultaneously in Canada by
Georg J. McLeod Limited, Toronto.

Printed and bound in the United States of America at the Haddon Craftsmen, Scranton, Penna.

Library of Congress Catalog Card Number 68-12155

FOR VIRGINIA
*without whom I might have lost the sense of wonder*

# Contents

# *Foreword*

T R I P L E   R I D G E   F A R M consists of one hundred
acres and lies in the southwest corner of Waushara County,
Richford Township, in central Wisconsin, where thousands
of years ago the Green Bay lobe of the glacier pushed up
hills of debris known today as the End Moraine.

"Why, that's the old John Wentland farm!" said our neighbor, Grandpa Fenske, when my husband went over to talk
to him about it. "You're not going to buy *that* hilly place!

9

There ain't more'n thirty acres of tillable land on the whole farm."

We admired Grandpa Fenske; he owned one of the best farms in the township, and he was a stable and honest man.

"Look at that road to his far east pasture," he continued. "Every rain narrows it, washing away the sides. If it wasn't for the oaks all over that hill, the road would have disappeared long ago. The soil is just sand, not worth planting."

When Henry and I talked about it, I said we could underplant the red and black oaks with red and white pines to control the erosion. We could put pines on the three hills, leaving the thirty acres of agricultural land free for crops.

"And, Dad," said our fifteen-year-old daughter, Virginia, "my horse could have the nicest pasture!" Along the Wedde Creek, which is the most important feature of the farm, runs a valley of perhaps twenty acres, used in the past century for pasturing cattle. "Trig could stay there alone during the week while we are in Madison; he'd have water and grass and could go back to his corral whenever he wished. Oh, Dad!"

"The stream is small," I said, "but the water is fast, and there's a lot of gravel for trout to spawn on . . ."

My professor husband has a "thing" about trout streams. Any piece of land that would interest him would have to contain a stream cold and fast enough for trout.

We bought the farm, to use on weekends and vacations, and this is the story of what it did for us and to us as well as of what we did to and for it. It became for us more than a piece of land, for it is a composite of atmosphere and concrete object, the sobbing cry of a bird as it rises from the water, a graceful scroll etched in snow by the wind, a quiet solitude, a warmth about the heart. We live with it and in it until it is part of us. That's why we like to be there, why we love it.

RUTH FOUTS POCHMANN

# Triple Ridge Farm

# I   *The Joy of Discovery*

DRIVING down a narrow, unfamiliar lane off Warren Road that first morning in April, I was aware of a feeling of expectancy and wariness. Earlier at Wichner's Store in Richford, Martha Wichner had told me about the property.

"I've been forgetting to tell you, Ruth," she had said, "about an abandoned farm three miles from here, the old John Wentland place. It's been for sale three or four years. It's got water, like your Henry wants."

Clara Berg, clerking for her brother Bill and her sister-in-law, added skeptically, "Mrs. Wentland nearly went crazy from lonesomeness. The farm's so far from the road."

Art Bruch's hired man, Ed, had good ears. "That Wedde Creek's small water at the farm," he offered, "but it's got trout, big uns, down where it runs under JJ." As he left the store, he called back to me, "Poachers sure like the place. They get fish and grouse out of season and shine deer in them hills."

The mention of trout led me to visit the farm before Henry could arrive for the weekend. His classes at the University in Madison would not be over until the following day. I could investigate alone and decide whether this place had potentiality for him and me and our fifteen-year-old daughter, Virginia. Water, flowing water, was the one characteristic our land must have, for trout-stream improvement was his chief interest. The opportunity to work on a stretch of water of his own was his reason for wanting to buy more land than surrounded our summer cabin on the Mecan River.

"Pines, Martha, are there any pines on that farm?" I had asked her, for room to plant pines and the privilege to watch them grow and to smell their fragrance were among my reasons for wanting to buy acreage.

"Yes, I think Mr. Wentland planted a good many before he left."

Now I was alone in this abandoned place, circling a low meadow rough with last summer's stalks of rue and joe-pye weed; ahead was a gentle slope wooded with white oak and white pine, no leaves yet on the oaks. I drove up the rise and braked so suddenly the motor died.

Before me lay the buildings, and it was as if I had awakened from a dream of them to find them real. They were arranged according to a sketch I had drawn a year before: farmhouse facing south, so that most of the rooms would catch the prevailing southwest breeze; barns and other outhouses to the east, so odors would not reach the house; and half-grown pine plantations all around, in groups of a hundred or so.

The house was colorless, having lost long ago whatever paint had once dressed it up, but it was not a skimpy house. It was the typical Wisconsin farmhouse at the turn of the century: T-shaped, with a veranda running across the front. A homey, friendly house. Even now, forlorn, unkempt, it welcomed me.

I was strangely shaken as I opened the door of my car (the "hearse," as Henry called my old Packard) and walked slowly to the wide concrete steps. They were broken in places, and squirrels had left piles of acorn caps there among the wet willow leaves. I rested a hip on the porch floor and swung my legs up. Better not risk falling through the steps, I thought.

Two doors opened from the porch, one to the kitchen, surely, and the other to the "front room," I hoped. Peering through the streaked and cloudy glass, I could make out a big Boston rocker. Through the other door, which was ornamented with applied scrolls of wooden leaves, I could see a chandelier of polished brass with six hurricane shades; beneath was a round parlor table on which was an object that appeared to be a stereoscope. An ornate metal-grille heater and a white wicker chair were the only other articles I could distinguish.

"That's good," I said to myself. "I can welcome guests on the porch and take them directly into my living room, not into the kitchen as everybody around here does!"

I laughed and jumped off the porch, noting that a walk made of large flat native sandstone led out to a yard pump beside a giant red oak.

I made mental notes: probably no water indoors; nice view from front porch and windows; good parking space between house and barns; beautiful red and white pines at rear of house; a quick drop then to a low meadow (my heart, too, made a note just there: a perfect place for a reflecting pool, which had long been in my plans, but about which I had not spoken); white oaks along a wide path or road running between the pines and the meadow (these oaks indicate the soil is good); and the ridge lines of the house roof straight, absolutely unsagging—Henry would ask first about that.

As I rounded the northwest corner of the house, I was startled by a great horned owl swooping down from the top of an oak to snatch something, possibly a luckless mouse, from the meadow floor and returning swiftly to his high limb to eat it. Four crows set up a picket line in the next oak and let him know in no uncertain terms that they vigorously objected to his action, and indeed to his very presence.

The silence had been so profound that their raucous cawing set my heart to beating faster. I considered inspecting the barn, but that should be Virginia's pleasant duty, I thought, since her saddle horse, Trig, would be its sole occupant. Perhaps Virginia and her Richford friend, Arla Mae Miller, would come with me after lunch to investigate this farm further.

With singing heart I drove back to the cabin on the Mecan and described the farm to Virginia.

"There'd be a barn for Trig, and good water, and a fine pasture, I'm sure."

"What's the stream like? Would Dad want it? No use in your getting excited over it if Dad won't like the creek." She continued currying Trig, though he was already shining like burnished copper.

"I haven't seen the stream. Will you and Arla Mae go with me after lunch to investigate it and the barn?"

Arla Mae lived about a quarter of a mile down the river road and was our most faithful visitor every weekend. Virginia had been only six years old when we bought the half acre on the Mecan and moved a lake cottage to our site. Arla would greet us each Friday with a joyful, "I seen youse when you turned in at the gate, and I hurried right over!" Ever since that first day she and Virginia had been bosom friends, playing together in the water, searching for fresh-water clams, pulling leeches off each other when they happened to attach themselves to one of their tender legs, helping Emil Wiesjahn look for his wayward white turkeys that preferred to nest in the wide-leaved skunk cabbage and lady fern of the riverbank; and, at Arla Mae's home, the girls gathered eggs in the chicken coop and shared thick slices of homemade bread fresh from Mrs. Miller's oven.

Now that Virginia owned a saddle horse, she could not spend as much time with Arla as she had before. She loved her solitary rides through the rolling countryside, and she liked time for dreaming. But she welcomed Arla's companionship for short periods of each day.

As soon as we had eaten, I took the girls with me, but when they saw the weather-beaten house they had nothing to say. I think they were embarrassed for me.

"You and Arla explore the barn," I suggested. "Decide which stall will be best for Trig and where you'll keep his hay. Look at the loft and see whether the floor is strong enough for you to have slumber parties up there."

Virginia rolled her eyes at me but said not a word. The two strolled lackadaisically across the yard and disappeared through the nearest barn door.

I tried all the openings on the porch, hoping to find an easy entry, but all were fast.

"No broken windows. That speaks well for the boys hereabout." I was again talking to myself. Through the cloudy glass I could see another object in the "front room"—a brass Aladdin lamp with a milk-glass shade.

This time, as I walked to the rear of the house, I noticed that the ground under the pines was littered with beer cans and whiskey bottles, lard cartons, and parts of an old bedspring. Heaps of debris led down to the sandy wagon road. But from that road north to a winding hedgerow, probably along the creek, I thought, the land was clean. Again my thoughts turned to a small lake right there, where it could be seen from the house all day. It could be a swimming pool in summer and an ice rink in winter; it would reflect the red beauty of the white oaks in October, and the house behind the pines; it would serve, too, to slow down the surface runoff after heavy rains and therefore save the banks of the stream.

The stream. I must see it. "God, let it be big enough to warrant Henry's interest," I whispered.

I walked down the wagon road for perhaps a hundred yards. I came to a bridge, but it looked unsafe. Worm fishermen had whacked holes in the planks so they could dangle their lines in the deep water beneath. Having been coached by Henry on how to approach a trout stream, I had come up slowly and peered beyond the bridge into a pool perhaps thirty feet wide. As I found the deep part, in the current, a dozen fish waved there, headed upstream, waiting for food to float toward them. I leaned forward, the better to see. The fish darted for the shadows near the banks. My heart leapt. The stream was larger than I had expected, and it had trout. Henry would be interested! Upstream from the bridge, alders and red-twig dogwood met over the water; that meant the channel was narrow and deep. Downstream, though, the channel ran through a large open pasture; the banks were naked and rough where they had lost huge chunks of soil during the Big Thaw. Cattle had trampled those banks for a hundred years. Henry would have plenty of opportunity to carry out his theories about soil conservation, watershed management, and stream improvement.

From the bridge I could see that sand covered most of the gravel bottom. Henry wouldn't like that, but the girls would. So I walked to the barn to get them.

High-pitched voices came from the loft.

"Hey, what are you doing?" I called. It was obvious they had found a broom and were sweeping, for through the wide cracks came a rain of dust and straw.

"Oh, Mother! It's grand up here!"

Virginia climbed down the difficult vertical ladder, sneezing from the dust. Arla followed. Both had red bandannas around their heads and across their faces.

"You must see it up there!" Virginia was ecstatic. "Soon's the dust dies down, you go up and look. And here, this is the horse stall. It was built for two horses. See the wooden floor? Trig would have loads of room. And over there is the calf stall, and this is the cow stall."

"Stanchion," corrected Arla. "Five stanchions. Sure is a little farm."

"Plenty big for Trig," declared Virginia. "He'll like the calf stall best; it opens into the corral. And, Mother, up there's the haymow. See how the hay's pitched down from the loft and then given to the calves through this opening? Isn't that convenient? Can I ride Trig over here tomorrow?"

I laughed. "We don't own the farm yet."

"I mean just ride him over for fun."

"All right. I'll come again too."

And come we did, early, though Henry was not to arrive before noon. In our eagerness we couldn't wait. Virginia, on Trig, cut through the Wiesjahns' tamaracks, over the Randalls' hills, and across the Fenskes' fields. It was a fine spring day, sunny and fresh, still cool enough for headscarf and jacket because of the customary April wind. I arrived ahead of her and walked to the bridge to wait. I saw her coming down the oak-covered hill behind the old Schroeder place and hoped she wouldn't fall into an open ruin of a cellar, where the house used to stand. Trig, a former race horse, was sure-footed, but lilacs had grown over the stone cellar walls, hiding them. I was relieved to see her stay close to the pine windbreak as she advanced.

I could see no fish in the bridge pool today. Maybe they had already eaten breakfast and were now resting under the watercress, which was beginning to get thick at the edges of the water.

Waiting, I marveled at the variety of terrain I had already seen. High and low, wet and dry, sandy and peaty, sloping, rolling, flat. The pH would range from very acid to neutral, I guessed, and that would mean an extraordinary number and variety of native flora. I had learned about pH during a wild year as a Girl Scout leader, trying vainly to teach nature lore to seventh-grade girls who were already more interested in human nature than in Mother Nature.

My thoughts returned to the stream when I saw a shadow stabilize itself in the swift water. A brook trout. Henry had told me the Wedde was one of the few streams left in Wisconsin cold enough and pure enough to house the brook trout, which seems to be more strict in its requirements than are rainbows and browns. Pasturing has ruined the cover on the banks of most creeks and rivers, causing the water to warm up and hiding places to disappear. The rainbows and browns, imported fish, are used to warmer temperatures than is the brook trout and so survive where the daintier brook cannot. I hoped Henry would feel and respond to the challenge to keep the Wedde cool and right for this species.

Virginia guided Trig through a broken-down fence along the Fenske line.

She called to me. "Mother, I'm going to see how large this pasture is and find out the condition of the fence."

With a gay wave, she put Trig into his canter and rode fence around the pasture.

The day before, after our return to our cabin, several cars had passed, the young drivers calling hello and blowing their horns at Virginia. She was very pleased by this rural friendliness, but her smile was followed by a frown.

"If we should move to the farm, Mother, nobody would ever ride by, for the house can't be seen from the road. Nobody I know ever goes in that direction; they all go west to Coloma or east to Wautoma."

For an hour then she had gone about her duties with Trig, watering, feeding, and currying him, but appearing very solemn. Then she had brightened and said, "It would be nicer for Trig, though. He'd be warmer in that stall, and cooler too, and he could go into it to escape the flies. He'd have water and grass whenever he wanted it, not just when I lead him to it."

Today she was as eager as I was to explore further. After an hour she appeared at the corral, filled with enthusiasm for the many pretty trails she had found. "And, Mother, there's another big pine plantation on the east boundary, over near Lackelts'. You'll love it. The pines there are old enough to have a deep carpet of needles."

After she had relieved Trig of his saddle and put him into the calf stall, "just to try it out," she fastened the corral gate and came to see what I had discovered in the buildings area.

"A real pioneer log house!" I said, pointing to a gray structure some three hundred feet south of the barn, and we walked over to it. An authentic log house it was, with one big room, perhaps sixteen by twenty feet, and a loft. "Up there's where the children slept, I guess. See, there are gable windows and a front dormer to make it comfortable."

We could see daylight through missing strips of mortar, and there was no floor.

Virginia climbed gingerly up a fragment of stairway made of short logs let into vertical two-by-twelves, but gave up the venture as too dangerous. "The roof looks like a sieve," she announced.

We later learned that John Wentland had built his first house and brought his bride here near the turn of the century. Three Wentland children were born in the log house; but after the family moved into the nice frame house, the old log structure was used for storing heater wood and as a stable.

We learned also that, though the acreage had been owned by various farmers since the War of 1812, when, as part of the Territory, it was given in payment for military services, only John Wentland had left his mark on the land. He had built well and had added humus to the light soil of his farm by digging in the quantities of oak leaves dropped in October and those forced off the branches by new leaves in May.

"Leaves are as good as boughten fertilizer," he told us when we visited him and his aged wife in Berlin to ask about the farm. But that came much later than this first April of our discovery.

For Virginia, this old home of the pioneers was not as much a thrill as the wire and tin-strip pen behind it. The lower part of the fence was of chicken wire, but the upper part was a twenty-four-inch strip of tin.

"That's to keep an animal from climbing out," said Virginia.

She knelt then and dug with her hands to see whether the wire went into the ground. "It does! That's to keep them from digging out."

A real fur farm it was, built, so a placard on the gate said, according to specifications laid down by the Wisconsin Conservation Commission. The enclosed area was about sixty feet by one hundred and contained two smaller wire pens with wire over the top as well as on the sides, and a red frame building with a chimney pipe protruding from the roof.

"It has windows too! Oh, Mom, I could have hens or pheasants or raccoons—just about any animal or bird could live here!"

"Happy would probably get it," I said, "at least at first. Henry would want him to have a place large enough to run in so he wouldn't be stiff when hunting season came around." Happy was Henry's Brittany spaniel. I couldn't imagine him content in a pen with caged birds, but it would certainly be a fine place for him alone. Mature red oaks shaded it on the south and west; on the east it was open to the sun. I would plant lilac and crab apple on the north, the side toward the farmhouse.

"Let's walk up the hill behind the barn," said Virginia, "to see the pines I told you of."

I retrieved a sack of apples from the car, and we walked up a wagon road in a shallow valley between the first and second ridges. There seemed to be three ridges, all running east to west and springing from one wide hill near County Road JJ, like the thumb and first two fingers of a hand, the northernmost ridge being the thumb, as it was shorter than the other two.

We found the pines handsome and healthy, about twenty feet tall, and mostly red pine, or Norway, with a few white pine around the outer edges. We found deer tracks in the sand and surmised the animals used the plantation for shelter at night. I breathed deeply of the exquisite fragrance and peered into the dim shade.

"We couldn't possibly walk through it now," I said. "The lower limbs make an impassable barrier. What fun it would be to prune a winding walk through the maze . . ."

To the south we came upon the "Dump." Every farm has one, and intriguing they are sometimes, having received discards for many, many years. However, our cursory examination yielded no antique glass or china, so we crawled under a three-strand wire fence and started downhill toward the stream.

A few steps later we both exclaimed in happy surprise. We were standing in a patch of white pasqueflowers. With everything else still so winter-dead, no green anywhere except the pines, these strikingly lovely blossoms were unbelievable. Each cupped flower was three inches across, even larger when I held the petals out. Their foliage was sparse and fernlike, hardly visible around the clustered blossoms rising only a few inches from the ground. I pinched off a leaf to identify positively in my Wherry's *Wild Flower Guide*; for pasques are rare nowadays, and I had seen them only once before. That time, as now, they grew on the very top of a high hill, partially shaded by oaks, and with a northern exposure. Later, when I was telling Bill Doege (Day) about it—Bill was a Wichner's Store regular—he said it was called windflower around those parts but that he knew of only three more hills where it grew, and not in profusion anywhere.

Virginia and I returned to the car by way of the top of Big Ridge, as we began to call this most precipitous hill. Though we had had several thrilling experiences already, we were due for another. From the open part just above the pines that ran up the steep slope from the barn, we came upon a tremendous view. We could see another part of the End Moraine, the section near Hancock, seven miles to the north. A quick study of a geographical map of the state the night before had shown me that the old Wentland place was situated in the moraine that had been pushed up by the glacier and extended in ridges north and south of us.

"There's the Coloma water tower." Virginia pointed west. "Aren't the windrows nice?"

They were. With fields still gray and beige, the long, straight streaks of green pines and spruce marking the north-south lines made a pretty picture indeed. The nearest farm, a half mile away, looked to me like a German village in the lower Alps, with the white house and red barns nestled in the side of a hill and the whole overcast with the purple of distance.

"Yes, it's the prettiest view I have seen in all Richford Township!"

Henry came at noon. Before he could leave his Ford, Virginia ran to tell him of the farm. I watched from the cabin window and saw him sitting, listening. The two brown heads were close together. He nodded once, then vigorously shook his head several times, and, as they walked toward the house, I heard him laughing at her. She abruptly turned away and went to Trig's small stall, her head bowed and her hands clasped behind her back.

"So you've just about bought the John Wentland place?" he said as he came in.

"Do you know the farm, Henry?"

"Sure. One of the poorest places in the area. It does have water, but not enough to work with. I've fished the Wedde—"

He had fished every flowing water in a radius of twenty miles.

"In the last five or six years?"

"No, I guess not in the last five. Didn't see the use of wasting my time."

"I saw a dozen brook trout in the pool just below the bridge."

"Yes, but that pool is the only one on the whole stretch. Below, on the Lackelt farm, there are more springs and much more water. Down by JJ it's really good."

"That's what Ed said. But I saw springs on the Wentland place too. Couldn't they be cleaned out and made to produce more? Let's go over there this afternoon and walk along the stream, all the way down, and see what it's really like. If it looks at all good in April, it'll be better later."

In the face of his skepticism I couldn't bring myself to talk about all the good features of the farm, but I could point them out, one by one, if we were strolling together. However, while I was preparing lunch, I decided not to go with him. After all, he had the right to discover and deserved the privilege of finding out for himself what the farm had to offer.

Soon after we had eaten our chicken soup and grilled cheese sandwiches, I said to him, "Henry, I could love that place; it fits our family better than anything else we've looked at. It has everything I have listed as a requirement, but it has to appeal to you as well as to me. So you go alone, as I did, and look for what you yourself want to find."

He was gone five hours!

I had begun to wonder whether he might have encountered some of those poachers and had his head bashed in. Then came his double "beep-beep," and I ran to meet him.

His mouth was turned down at the corners and his lips pushed out, his brow furrowed. "I walked all the way downstream and didn't see a fish. There just aren't any trout. The whole stream bed is badly silted in except above the bridge, where cattle have been kept out.

"The house would need as much work as building a new one would. The porch floor would have to be replaced. The front steps and back ones are broken; so is the concrete floor of the back inset porch, where stove wood has been pitched in carelessly. There's no water indoors. The tin roof is rusty, one of the chimneys is broken down, storm windows would have to be bought, also screens, everything needs paint." He paused for a breath. "It would cost a fortune to make it comfortable.

"The soil is worn out. Didn't you notice there is no grass in the yard or barnyard? If grass won't grow, nothing else will.

"The farm does have flowing water, but—no, it wouldn't be worth my effort to bring that stream back."

We didn't mention it again that evening, and we went to bed early, each with his own thoughts.

Virginia was up at six for a sunrise ride on Trig.

I ate alone and went outdoors to rake leaves off the plan-tain lily, which was sending up reddish spears. I had lain awake for a good part of the night and had done some hard thinking. This morning I felt clearheaded. The Wentland farm was the one we should buy, but I was resigned to waiting. Henry is a cautious man, and he was weary of desk work after eight months of lecturing and writing, so weary that the prospect of much physical work in the restoration of an old house tired him more. I had warned Virginia not to nag her father. "He'll probably come around to our way of thinking eventually. But if we push him, he'll resist. Be patient."

After breakfast Henry put on his short rubber boots and said he was going to explore a spot on the Mecan down by the old dam below the Richford bridge. Trout season would not open for another two weeks, but he wanted to see whether the river had been stocked. It was customary for the Conservation Department to bring milk cans full of young rainbow and German brown trout from the state hatcheries and let them out at the bridge on Highway 21, at the Richford bridge on County Trunk B, and at the Break-fast Pool, off one of the town roads.

"I may go down to the Breakfast Pool to have a look around," he called back to me as he drove off.

I nodded and waved. He'd go again to the farm, I thought. When he had not returned by noon, I was fairly certain he had.

"Don't get your hopes up," I said to Virginia, but both she and I laughed light-heartedly.

At one-thirty he came. Though Virginia and I had eaten, we sat at the table watching him and hanging on his every word. He kept a solemn face as he talked and ate, and he tried not to let us see that he knew how eager we were.

"The Mecan has been well stocked," he reported. "Harlan Beutler and Frank Wieland were at the bridge too, checking. I asked them about farms for sale around here. Harlan said that when farms with water were known to be for sale, the neighboring farmers bought them before they could be advertised. I asked him why the Wentland place had not sold. Frank said it was a poor farm, too hilly and too swampy for a man to make a living on.

"But I went over there again," he went on, "to look at the stream. I can see it has possibilities—I saw quite a few trout this morning, small ones. Planting the banks would in time help the stream clean itself of the silt."

Virginia caught her breath. I spoke softly, "If there are little ones, surely there must be some big ones."

"Yes, I guess there's some spawning going on there in the fall. Worm fishermen have made holes in the bridge planks so they can sit there and wait for the trout to take their worms! An unspeakable practice!"

A dry-fly fisherman, he had little use for the lowly worm man.

"Martha said the owner will come back for the opening of trout season. Would you like to talk to him? Ask questions about the stream? And find out what he's asking for the farm?"

"It will have to be mighty cheap. That house is in awful shape."

So he *was* thinking about it as a possibility for us!

"Whoopee!" shouted Virginia, and ran from the room.

I laughed, and Henry vouchsafed a grin, as he watched her head for Trig's stall.

"I noticed the ridge of the roof is straight," I said, "and there's a new paint on the market for tin roofs; it's supposed to cover rust and prevent its spread."

He was surprised. "You mean you wouldn't want a new roof?"

"I like tin roofs in the country. Rain sounds good on a tin roof, and it's good protection from fire."

Virginia came running back. "Dad, did you go into the barn?"

"Yes, and somebody's been cleaning the loft."

"Arla and I swept the hay into one corner and leveled it so we can have a slum—" her voice trailed away, and she looked at me for advice about finishing her sentence. I smiled— "slumber party up there if we buy the farm. It's a swell place. And did you see the nice stall that opens into the corral? It's big enough for Trig, and he likes it already. And did you see the nice pen for Happy? Gee, Dad, he could really have himself a ball, digging holes and chasing squirrels."

Henry looked at her skeptically. "And did you see the pasture fence needs mending in a dozen stretches, and would you be willing to help mend it? Fixing fence is hard work." He sighed. "There's enough work to be done on the house alone to keep a dozen men busy, and I'm just a professor, not a carpenter."

I spoke with studied calm. "We could do most of it ourselves, don't you think? You've always been clever with your hands, and I'm willing. There'd be no reason for getting it done in one or even two seasons. We could live here in the cabin-on-the-Mecan while we work over there at the house-on-the-Wedde."

I slipped away during the afternoon, with my camera, and took some colored slides of the lovely pasqueflowers and the buildings. It would be good to compare the "before" and "after" pictures, I told myself.

I was not that certain of the eventual purchase, but I was enjoying the pleasant excitement of hope and anticipation. Back at the cabin, though, I was silent. Too silent, Henry said. He knew my thoughts were on the farm; so even if I did not nag him about it, I was exerting pressure anyway.

We returned to Madison Sunday afternoon, as usual. The next weekend Henry went to Richford without Virginia and me, she having a date in town for her class dance. When he came home that Sunday night, I was bursting to ask whether he had gone again to the farm, but he kept me in suspense until after dinner. Then as he lay on the sofa, resting, he called me to him.

"Do you honestly think that's the right one for us?"

I could only nod.

"Well, I can see its possibilities. Let's see the owner next weekend. I got his name and address from the Coloma People's Bank."

I hugged him. "What made you decide?"

"Well, I went over there twice yesterday, and each time I came up on a poacher. One man was hunting grouse, and one was shooting trout."

"*Shooting trout!*" I was horrified.

"Yes, with a thirty-thirty. He shot into the water under the bridge to stun the fish, then lifted them out by hand. He had ten fish—ten to twelve inches each—in his bucket when I came on him, and was lifting out a three-pounder, one that had remained after last fall's spawning, I guess."

We bought the farm.

# II  *That First Summer*

"'I T ' S a lifetime job," said Henry as he sipped hot tea from
his thermos bottle while we were resting on the yard-pump
platform. He had been cleaning the debris from around the
house, had taken three trailer-loads of it to the Dump, and
had another load ready to go.

"We can do it. I can't think of a better job, can you? We'll
be beautifying while we're restoring, and we'll be in fresh
air most of the time." I took a deep breath. "It's the best air
I've smelled since leaving Texas twenty years ago!"

"Humph!'

34

"You mustn't stop fishing and hunting, Henry. Take off some time every day to fish so you'll enjoy the work you're doing on the stream."

We were sleeping at the cabin on the Mecan, eating breakfast and dinner there, but working all day at the farm. Sometimes we ate our lunch under the lone oak atop Big Ridge, so we could absorb the long view while we rested. Often the three of us would snooze a bit in the soft grasses after filling our eyes with the green-and-blue pattern of near and distant fields and woodlands. And when we waked, I, for one, had a deep spiritual content.

Ownership of land is a steadying thing. We felt our responsibility toward our acreage, not from an economic point of view, but from an ethical one. In our case we did not intend to raise crops for profit—at least not in the early years; we wanted to conserve the depleted resources, and restore them where necessary, in order to make up for the neglect and lack of foresight over the years.

When making our plans on paper, we aimed at letting the fields make a comeback in fertility, at giving a new opportunity to the three dry hills to grow a forest, at preventing destruction to the stream by cattle and floods, and at making an attractive habitat for the little animals and birds, as well as for the trout.

We decided that the restoration of the house, the planting of the pines, and the stabilizing of the stream banks should have priority that first summer. So, even before the final papers had been signed, we went to the county seat in Wautoma and talked with the Conservation Department men, the district managers of soil, water, and wildlife. They were helpful and enthusiastic.

Mr. Norbert Damaske, wildlife manager at that time (later manager of the State Game Farm in Poynette), gave us several bundles of leftover shrubs to put along the creek. Though the shrubs were free, few farmers could be persuaded that year to give up corners and unused stretches of land to such plants, for they had just finished cleaning up those sections to comply with the fairly new idea of "clean farming," which had been advocated by some researchers in agriculture. The latter had advised farmers to cut down or kill by spraying all the shrubs and vines that made fence rows; as the farmers cut, they destroyed shelter and nesting places, runways, and even food for wildlife.

Harold Fenske was one of the few farmers who realized their mistake.

"Heck!" he said. "Birds destroy more insects than these commercial sprays do, and they're cheaper. I'm going to let my fence rows come back."

That first April, Norbert and his helper, Jones, brought many shrubs to us and planted them in the right places, telling us why they selected each site. Bittersweet vines require rather dry places in the sun if they are to bear their spectacular red berries with yellow bracts. Highbush cranberry, on the other hand, requires partial shade and some moisture if it is to look like a trimmed Christmas tree all winter, with its large drooping clusters of soft red berries. Wild crab apple likes sun, about seven hours of it daily, and moisture. Black haw will do well at the edge of dry fields.

All together there were more than a thousand plants. We were delighted. They were, of course, very small—some only six inches high; as soon as the grass grew to maturity, I couldn't see many of them, but I cultivated those I could find, to give them a better chance. During dry months I watered the ninebark and cranberry, which were conveniently near the stream. By the third season these two shrubs were giving us blossoms, and on the wild grape long tendrils reached for fence posts and saplings.

Each April for four or five years we obtained plants from the state nurseries and planted them according to instructions sent with them. A hundred mountain ash trees went into well-drained, but not dry, partly shaded spots; fifteen hundred wild crabs went along the north bank of the stream.

"How can one plant fifteen hundred crabs without adding beauty to the landscape?" I mused, remembering we had had to sign a statement that these state plants would not be used for landscaping privately owned property.

Two hundred bush honeysuckles went near the pond, which was built the first fall, and are now a bird-inhabited thicket. We made big brush piles for rabbits and quail and planted "wild" lilac (*Syringa villosa*) around them.

By 1960 the demand for these shrubs became so great that the Conservation Department had to contract with privately owned nurseries for supplementary supplies, and then a small charge had to be made for them.

Hearing that wild plum was about to become extinct in certain sections of the country, we bought several hundred and planted them to form thickets near the water and the pines. We, as well as the cedar waxwings and towhees, like plums.

Henry and I decided to experiment with some plants that have not been thought hardy for central Wisconsin. We established a plat on the east slope of Jackpine Hill, and there he ran a furrow with his new plow and tractor. We put in a double row of multiflora roses about a foot apart, and the plants six inches apart in the row. Henry put some also into the steep eroded bank about halfway downstream. In both locations the roses grew apace, those on the bank doing better. Some that we planted in more open exposures were winterkilled when the temperature dropped to thirty-five degrees *below* zero, then went up to thirty-three degrees *above* zero, and back to seven *below*.

It may be surprising to residents of more temperate climates to know that the intense cold is not the usual killer of plants; it is the continual freezing and thawing, freezing and thawing, alternating for five and one-half months, that ruins the flora. Our winter sun is very warm, doubly so because of the reflection from the snow, so that it is possible to have a wide variation of temperature within twenty-four hours. In foundation plantings one can use winter protection, such as marsh hay or leaves, but at Triple Ridge we test for unprotected hardiness.

"No use to plant fancy roses up here," Henry told me when I put in a Peace rose and some of the Radiance varieties. He was right. All died the first year. The "sub-zero roses," though, grew well enough to be a delight to me; they sometimes die down to the ground during the winter, but they will grow again and bloom for me during the season. Such old-fashioned roses as the Rugosas and their descendants, the Grootendorsts, and the moss roses do very well. They need only to be severely pruned each June, for some of their thick stems die, characteristically.

"Let's try some peaches," I said.

"They won't live," said my pessimist.

Again he was right. They lived for a few years but never did grow into trees or bear fruit. It was not the cold this time; it was the soil.

While all of us worked daily on the house, each of us had his own particular field of interest. Besides her spirited bay, Virginia's, this first summer, was a series of zoological experiments concerning a pair of fancy black pigeons, five laying hens, and native fishes in a home aquarium.

Trig had learned Virginia's ways so well that he obeyed the bend of her body, and she understood his reactions to strange objects so that she could quell his fear by speaking softly to him. They loved each other. It was a joy to see them silhouetted in the late afternoon as Trig cantered home along the top of one of the ridges.

"She seems 'growed' to him," said Henry.

The black pigeons built a nest and laid eggs in one of the wire pens in the fur farm, but something, perhaps a weasel, slipped through the wire and ate the eggs. Twice. So her breeding experiment with them was a failure, but all of us enjoyed watching them preen themselves and spread their remarkable tails.

The laying hens were amazing. Virginia had gone to Lauretta Schroeder to get them.

"I want to buy five hens, Mrs. Schroeder, that you think will continue laying all this summer."

"Sure, Virginia. You can pick 'em. Any five."

Virginia looked closely at the White Leghorns, which were nervous now with strangers about.

"That one looks good. Red wattles, white feet. Can you catch her?"

Lauretta aproned that one into a corner of the yard and easily caught her. Virginia took the hen gently and turned her up to look under her tail.

"Large vent," she said approvingly.

One by one she chose four others, and all five were placed in a large carton on the back seat of the "hearse." Lauretta was amused, as was I, and she was pleased that Virginia had chosen her hens from among the many available in Richford Township.

Virginia had read a poultry book on new feed; so we drove to the Follett and Leach Feed Mill in Coloma, where she bought a sack or two—to the ill-hidden amusement of Arnold Schubert, the clerk.

"You're going to have a farmer in the family yet," he said to me, winking.

"I'll buy all your eggs," I told her on the way back to the farm, "at Madison prices."

Virginia kept up to date with the price and kept books on the daily production. In two months those five hens laid fourteen dozen huge white eggs! Astonished, I asked Lauretta whether her hens normally laid that well.

"Land sakes, no!" She laughed. "But in small lots hens always lay better'n big lots. Hens is too nervous and neurotic. They get excited easy. If a few can be kept quiet, they lay fine."

Virginia cautioned us not to speak loudly or move rapidly when we were near the chickens. She called each by name: Martha, Clara, Lauretta, Enid, and Josephine. Enid was the champion, accounting for fifty of the hundred and sixty-eight eggs.

"It's the cool water," Virginia explained. "I keep fresh cool water in five pans, see? Eggs are about two-thirds water, and more than half a hen's body is water. It seemed logical to me that a hen should want to drink often.

"And," she went on, "liquids soften the feed in her crop and aid her digestion and keep her cool in hot weather."

"You've convinced me," I said, "but I'm about broke!"


In July Henry bought a cultivator. "If you're to have a garden," he said to me, "I'll need this and the plow to prepare the soil for you."

I sat beneath an ancient Wolf River apple tree and watched the tractor tires crush the brittle stubble where cabbages used to form their tender rosettes. The green turf turned to black peaty loam as the iron point of the plow shoved through the four years' growth since the plat was last used, turning a rich, moist furrow.

"This is the best soil on the farm," called Henry.

That was to be expected, for farmers take good care of their garden spots, manuring them, raking in leaves, digging in wood ashes, and spreading bone meal. This specific place was parallel with our driveway, lower than the buildings area, in full sun. Its soil was a mixture of sand from the hills and peat from the valley, with a pH of seven. Turning under the grass and weeds now would be fine for adding humus and nitrogen. July was, of course, too late to plant seeds in this climate, but I planned to bring soon some wild asparagus from the field edges and from the roadside at our gate and make a permanent asparagus bed here in the garden, near enough to the house for me to water the plants with a garden hose. At that time farmers' wives in the area did not use water hoses, for they had no outdoor faucets.

In late August I did make the bed. As I was planting the last asparagus, Mr. Ed Warren, our nearest neighbor to the west, came walking up our drive.

"Oh, you're a month too early, miss. September's the time to move sparrowgrass," said this octogenarian.

"I intend to keep it wet. See? My water hose reaches to the edge of the garden."

I walked over to it and released the water.

"Oh! You've got a irrigated garden!"

After plowing the garden spot that day in July, Henry got down from his tractor, exercised his arms by pretending to be a windmill, then turned to the tractor and stroked its hood. "This will be my hired man," he said. I got the feeling that to own a tractor had been a secret longing of his while tied for years to a desk—like mine for a body of water, for swallows to skim across.

In August he bought a disk.

Fritz Sheley helped him assemble that disk. Fritz was one of nine friends who helped us that summer. Most of them were our guests on weekends, when they would undertake certain paint jobs, but Fritz was there more often, whenever we had several days of vacation. He was always ready for anything that burst upon us. He helped Virginia take up the six congoleum rugs, nailed one on top of the other on the kitchen floor; he aided me by slapping cloths, wet with tri-sodium sulphate, on the upstairs beams that were sticky with creosote running down the leaky chimney. The task of dissolving that smelly creosote and scraping it off the wood was the most unpleasant job we tackled throughout the restoration of the house. There would have been no use in covering it with Sheetrock, for in time the sticky stuff would have seeped through. So he and I tediously softened it and scraped it onto newspapers, which we burned in the big iron range.

Fritz painted Henry's workshop. One day he found that his head, as he stood on the ladder, was within inches of a wasp's nest, which was covered with inhabitants of a very active and suspicious nature. He fairly flowed down that ladder.

"I'm gittin' out o' here quicker'n skim milk comes through a tow sack!" Fritz was from Texas, but his was the Tennessee kind of humor, quick and unexpected in metaphor and simile. For years after he had returned to Texas, we quoted him.

One day I walked up quietly behind him while he was sitting on the bank, fishing.

"Are they biting?" I asked.

"If they are, they're biting themselves," said he, sotto voce.

At table one evening he said he had been eating too much

of Virginia's cooking and preferred to have just a doughnut hole without sugar, a sparrow neck, some mosquito knuckles, and perhaps pine-needle tea. He was what Martha Wichner called "a case."

Bryan Davis was another Texan who helped paint our house. He and Fritz, sons of friends of our courtship days, were now graduate students at the University of Wisconsin. They understood our situation and were willing to help us work in return for the weekends in the country. Their help was considerable, and we became fond of them.

Alden and Kay White were Madison friends who advised and appreciated and painted. Kay and I worked on the red siding, and Alden did the white trim while Henry made the window screens. Their son, Ray, helped Henry rebuild the plank bridge, and heavy work it was. Wearing rubber waders, they heaved big rocks into place and rested solid logs on them. Across the logs went the two-by-twelves. It grew into a sturdy structure, allowing the Fenskes' huge tractor to cross on it.

Virginia's classmates, Jeanne Larson and Gretchen Ihde, took turns riding Trig and cleaning out a spring, which later was incorporated into Birch Pool. Gretchen and Virginia repainted the red corncrib and rabbit hutch.

By the end of that first summer Triple Ridge was looking well-groomed. All the buildings had one coat of fresh red barn paint with white trim, the lawn was well defined by the driveway, and the parking area was clean and seeded to grass. With his tractor Henry had thrown up a shallow ridge behind the workshop and granary to shunt rain water behind the pines and away from the driveway in order to prevent the bad washouts we suffered after some of the storms.

One had been particularly disastrous. When Damaske and Henry were down by the bridge, deciding where to plant a thousand ninebarks, a storm had come up so suddenly that the men were drenched before they could race to the house.

"This is a dilly!" said Damaske, laughing, as he grabbed a porch post and swung himself up.

"The wind is straight out of the west," said Henry, "and it's very dark beyond the hill."

As I had earlier heard a tornado warning over the radio, I ran upstairs to see whether a funnel was visible on the horizon. There was none, but I didn't go down right away, for I was fascinated by what I saw. The willows and oaks were bending closer to the ground than I had ever seen them, and good-sized limbs were sailing down the driveway parallel with the ground. Sheets of white rain also were horizontal, seeming not to touch the earth at all.

Downstairs, from the kitchen window I saw these sheets crash against the barn, a white explosion, some rain going up and some going down, and willow limbs were strewn all over the parking area.

"What a mess!" Henry was thinking of the cleanup to be done.

I heard rain splashing down the tin stovepipe and thought it queer that I should hear that small inside noise when the outside tumult was so great.

The wind subsided before long, but a heavy rain fell for several hours. Damaske went home, the day wasted for him.

"Well, let's get busy," Henry said when our little world was quiet again.

We went to his workshop and each armed himself with his favorite implement—the rake for Virginia, the light shovel for me, and the heavy fork for Henry.

"Lucky the car was in the shed," Henry observed. "These limbs would have broken the windshield."

We picked up and raked up the branches and twigs, filling the trailer several times. And we shoveled sand on the driveway wherever it had been washed away.

Just before sunset time, clouds showed their silver linings, a glow broke over the farm, the clean leaves sparkled, and the air was deliciously fragrant.

But on another April day a similar storm did not leave central Wisconsin as quickly or as lightly damaged.

On April 3, 1956, a tornado alert was broadcast during a heavy rain at noon, but a bad wind did not hit us until shortly after two o'clock, when oval hailstones as large as robins' eggs accompanied it.

"This one is coming from the east," said Henry. "It may be a bad one. One thing is sure: we'll have no snow left by tomorrow."

When we had arrived that morning, about eighteen inches of snow had covered the hills, and the ice on the pond had showed no sign of melting except for a grayish color over the spring.

"It's high time for the Big Thaw," said Henry. And it was, for usually we have it in mid-March.

Now the thaw was upon us and in a dangerous way, for the snow melted all at once, that is, within a few hours, resulting in torrents rushing down the steep hills. From Big Ridge and Middle Ridge it gushed upon us as if a floodgate had been opened.

Henry paced back and forth from the front doors to the east windows. "Where there's sod and where the ground is still frozen, no damage is being done, but we'll have no driveway left."

"How'll we get out?" wailed Virginia.

Her father shrugged his broad shoulders. "Swim."

"Mother?"

"Oh, I think we can drive back of the pines and through

the fields if we can't use the driveway. Washouts in the alfalfa are unlikely. Once we reach Warren Road we'll have no trouble getting to Richford."

"Hey!" called Henry from the rear window. "Come and see what's happening to the pool."

We saw with fearful dismay that the ice had melted around the edges and was rising in a sheet as the water level rose. At the beginning of the storm about four feet of bank could be seen above the ice. In two hours the water had risen to within six inches of the top!

"Oh, I wish we had put in an outlet pipe!" I said.

"Those banks are tight with turf," Henry comforted me. "Even if the water were to go over, it probably wouldn't wash away much soil, and even if it did, it wouldn't mean the loss of the pool, for it's a dug pond, not dammed. The normal amount of water would remain with us, bank or no bank." And then, as if to himself, he said, "It would mean a lot of tractor work for Henry."

Suddenly the storm was over, and we went out to survey the damage. Extending from the house to the garden, a distance of about one hundred and fifty feet, the driveway was a gully three feet deep and four feet wide! Beyond the garden the culvert was washed out and the pipe lay exposed and broken.

Without a word Henry walked into the alfalfa field and looked about.

"I think we can make it through here," he said.

We left then for the cabin at Richford, too discouraged to start any repair work that day. As we drove through our gate, I switched on the car radio, and we learned that Berlin, Wisconsin, had been hit by a tornado, which had killed and injured an unknown number of people, had destroyed about thirty houses, and had damaged many more.

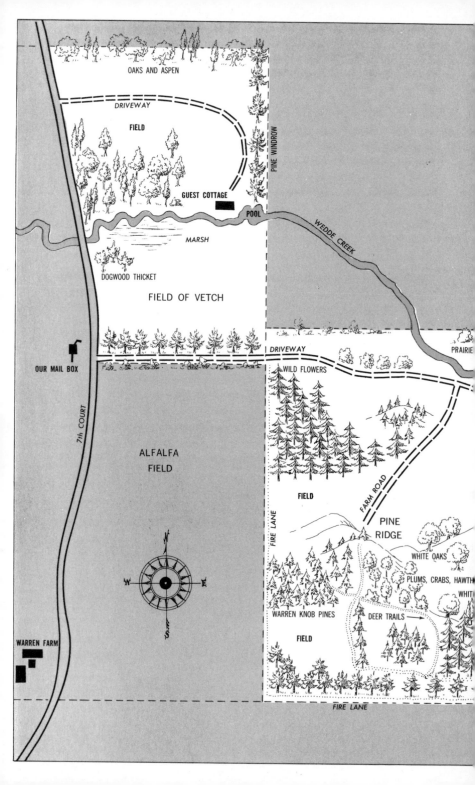

# TRIPLE RIDGE FARM

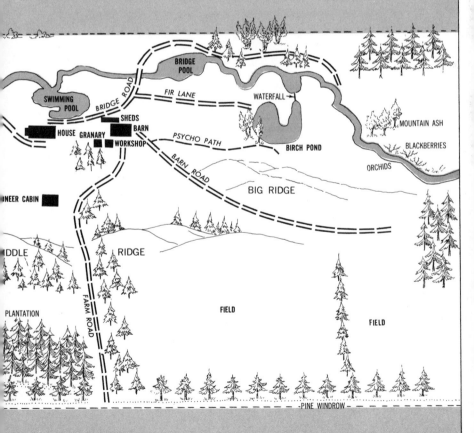

FENSKE FARMLAND

BRIDGE POOL

SWIMMING POOL

BRIDGE ROAD

FIR LANE

WATERFALL

MOUNTAIN ASH

SHEDS

HOUSE GRANARY BARN

WORKSHOP

PSYCHO PATH

BIRCH POND

BLACKBERRIES

ORCHIDS

BARN ROAD

BIG RIDGE

NEER CABIN

DDLE

RIDGE

FARM ROAD

PLANTATION

FIELD

FIELD

PINE WINDROW

FRAVEL AND SAWIN FARMLAND

"So that was it!" I said. "Our storm was part of that same turbulence. Well, I guess we're lucky after all; the tornado's force died out before it reached us. We got mostly water."

"Let's stop at Wichner's Store," said Virginia. "Bill will know all about it."

At the store there was much excitement. June Matz had talked by telephone with her sister in Berlin, learning that she and her family were safe and that her sister, seeing the tornado sling a five-month-old baby into a mud bank, had been able to extract the mud from the baby's nostrils and mouth in time to save his life.

The Wichners' telephone rang constantly; Richford people were calling to tell Bill and Martha that friends and relations in and around Berlin were safe or injured or dead. Wichner's Store was, as usual, the headquarters in time of disaster. Herb Pomplum hurried in; Herb was the man everybody depended on to keep the roads in shape.

"There have been two bad washouts," he told us. "One's down JJ."

We knew it was not along the stretch we had just come over, so it must be farther south, nearer Triple Ridge.

"You may need help," said Henry. "Bill, I've got a shovel in my car. Can you lend us another?"

We three then followed Herb to the place, intending to help him put up a warning notice and a barricade, but we were too late. The soil had been washed out from under the blacktop, and Milton Schwarzenska's car had broken through. Several men had already pulled it from the gaping hole. Milton had miraculously escaped injury, but the hood of his Ford had been torn off and the front axle broken.

Darkness was falling rapidly now, and the danger of a repetition of this accident was eminent. Herb gave directions to several men, and soon a lantern was lighted and hung in the center of the road on a barricade made of sawhorses. Herb was anxious about the other washout that had been reported. His wife, Wilma, had seen it and told him it was "as large as the Matzes' two-story house."

Later that night a driver disregarded Herb's hastily placed sign, BRIDGE OUT, and drove around the placard, saying to his seven passengers, "Know there ain't no bridge on this road." He and his little granddaughter were killed.

The next morning we put on long underwear beneath our usual heavy slacks and parkas, for we knew we'd be outdoors many hours in the April wind. We drove the three miles to the farm, going in through the field as we had come out the night before. Howard Fravel, a high-school senior who lived a mile south of our farm, was standing at the culvert.

"Knew you'd need me," he said.

While he and Henry threw our entire stock of fence posts into the gully, I went into the house and made a good fire in the iron range. Virginia brought more stove wood in a bushel basket to replenish the fire; then the two of us set about cutting pine branches, the only other material available in quantity, to lay on top of the posts before Henry packed in scoops of sand with the tractor.

As the driveway once again became usable, we cheered up somewhat, and all enjoyed a pot of vegetable-and-beef soup I had let cook slowly for hours on the range.

Afterward we walked around the pool, marveling that the banks had remained intact. Henry stood on the revetment he had made to shunt surface water into it.

"I'll lower that a little," he decided. "Some of the water in emergencies such as this should be allowed to go into the stream."

As a result of that harrowing experience Henry made several other changes, which have worked remarkably well in preventing a recurrence of driveway damage. He deepened the shallow ditch he had made earlier behind the workshop to divert the water from the barn road. He and Howard rolled the big logs bordering my flower beds into a position nearer the drive to allow more water to go south of it. He asked Herb Pomplum to bring truckloads of gravel for the drive when he built a new culvert for us. And all of us planted pines in deep furrows that Henry had plowed into the west side of Middle Ridge. The furrows slowed the runoff in that area, benefiting both the driveway and the pool as well as holding the topsoil.

One day some lines of Walt Whitman came to me as I strutted across the meadow, shovel on my shoulder, Happy panting at my side, and Trig following us inquisitively:

We, a curious trio, picking, wandering on our way,
Through these shores amid the shadows, apparitions pressing,
Pioneers! O pioneers!

I smiled and fell to wondering. Apparitions indeed! I had learned from our papers—patents and deeds—that this land was given as bounty for services rendered in the War of 1812 to one Orderly Sergeant Warren Frailing. In 1855 a John W. Bassett bought it from the United States Government; it had apparently reverted because of unpaid taxes. In 1861 he sold the west forty acres to Jasper L. White and the east forty to David Davis. Five months later Davis sold his to White's wife. The deeds were signed by Abraham Lincoln. In 1884 the Whites let their son Frank have the eighty acres, and he kept them until he sold to John Wentland and his bride, Alma, in 1904.

I turned to look again at the reflection in the newly dug pool of the red and white house topped by oak-covered hills. Reflected also was the chokecherry thicket, which in May had fringed the Wildwood with its white lace. The Wentlands couldn't have chosen a nicer spot on which to build.

I felt deeply gratified as I left the house one September morning to walk the half mile to our gate and the mailbox.

Watching for a possible new flower to press and studying the graceful flight of a Swainson's hawk above the poplars, I didn't look at the Warren farm, which recently had been sold to Philip Sawin of Madison. Not until I reached the sand-and-gravel road and pulled from the rural mailbox a welcome *Ford Times* magazine did I glance over toward the Sawin buildings.

I stopped dead in my tracks! Only that morning the barn had been a weathered gray, the same color as that of the several outbuildings ringing it, and the once-white farmhouse, needing paint, had been streaked with brown. But now, in less than a day, all the buildings stood brightly, brilliantly painted.

How could that be? For three months nine of us had labored at ours. For a while I stood there, staring. The house was a soft white, lovely against the green of three mature white pines. The barn, twice the size of ours, was red, or was it orange? I cocked my head at it.

"Ours is a nicer red!" I said aloud. I was belligerent in both attitude and thought. Jealous? Would we have wanted to forgo all the fun and companionship of the summer while we painted Triple Ridge? Even if we had had the money to hire it done? I grinned then and trudged back to the farmhouse to relay the news.

"Yeah," said Henry as he pumped water on his dirty hands and dried them on his khaki pants. "It was done in three hours, sprayed on, and cost eight hundred dollars."

Virginia and Fritz whistled. "Whew!" said Virginia. "How much did ours cost, Dad?"

"Mostly sweat," said he.

Sometimes we felt we had undertaken too much for inexperienced city folk, but we kept at it, buoyed often by such experiences as mine with the great blue heron.

I had watched that heron stand on the bank of the swimming pool by the hour, as still as a statue except for his eyes, which searched every inch of the bank and near meadow for a mouse or a frog.

"Some day," I thought, "I'm going to be near when you come; I'm going to see whether you're as beautiful as the bird book says."

But the opportunity was slow in coming. Each time I slipped out of my kitchen door, intent on creeping up on him, he'd lift his feathered beauty and be on his way to the rookery at the headwaters of the Mecan River about five miles away. Time after time I tried to fool him, but always he outsmarted me.

Then one day I outwitted him. I had been gathering watercress in the pool just below the bridge and was resting beneath a paper birch, which leaned over the water, hiding me.

The heron came gliding down, like a fragment of the blue sky, and lit in the shallow gravel run, just around the bend in the stream. On my hands and knees I crept across the bridge; once on my path between the ninebark bushes, I arose enough to waddle rapidly toward the willow. I could see him slowly walking downstream, intent on finding a young trout under the opposite bank, his blue head and long yellow bill pointed downward.

Counting on the gurgle of the water to prevent his hearing me, I crawled forward under the willow until I was lying parallel with a log not more than eight feet from His Majesty himself.

Literally holding my breath, I took in his brilliance and dignity and unbelievable height. With bent head he stood three feet tall. His neck was pink and purple, and his wings blue with a dark-red streak on the shoulders. He took another slow step or two forward, then turned to look under my bank, stretching his supple neck to increase his height to four feet! For a fraction of a second we stared at each other; then with only a soft "whoosh" he was gone, his wide wings fanning my face.

I lay still for several minutes.

"That was worth all the work to date," I whispered to the willow.

# III  *Restoration of the House*

T H E second summer we worked every day at the farm, for Henry did not teach in summer school that year. We still slept at our cottage on the Mecan and ate two meals there, but we spent from ten to twelve hours at the farm, with little regard for the clock.

As I now consider the whole restoration of the farm-house, it seems that our biggest mistake was in trying to put in the plumbing system without professional help. It would have been far less expensive in money, labor, time, and disposition had we hired plumbers from Wautoma or Plainfield. As it was, we had Fred Buschke, the only plumber in Coloma, for one week only. And sometimes we had Howard Fravel and a retired farmer in Richford, Walter Kapp. Henry and I did the major part of the job.

As I knew nothing about pipes and wrenches, nuts and bolts, I was merely errand girl and ditchdigger, and I fretted. Henry too was irritated with himself because he so often did the wrong thing. We snapped at each other. If the venture were ever in danger, it was then. I doubt that either of us would have let the restoration fall through, but our spirits dropped low for a while. If we had been less determined and stubborn, the bathroom might never have become a reality. But we lived through it, and we learned a lot.

Our bathroom pieces came from the old Eagles Club in Madison, which was being torn down to make room for the new Dane County Office Building, and the price was only thirty dollars for the three pieces.

"They're larger than modern sets and just as spotless as new ones," Henry told me after he had bought them.

"Does the tub have feet?" I asked.

"I'm afraid so."

"Good. That type is more in keeping with the house. I'll paint the outside of it red."

"Red!" He sounded scandalized.

"Yep. Red tub, red chair, white walls. Like 'um?"

"Doesn't matter, I guess. But I've never seen a red tub."

Decorating the rooms fell to me, and I thoroughly enjoyed the painting, wallpapering, and even the plastering. When the Wentlands occupied the house, the three downstairs bedrooms were quite small, allowing for little besides a double bed and a dresser. One of these, a room about seven feet by ten, became our new bathroom. Though the old-fashioned tub required as much room as a single bed would have, it left sufficient space for a three-drawer dresser and a red iron "ice-cream parlor" chair. Thus the bathroom became also a dressing room.

Henry chose for his bedroom the small one north of the living room, which has the same view the bathroom has. It overlooks the rock garden and wall, part of the Wildwood, the swimming pool, the meadow, and the poplar woods and Fenske's fields. He sleeps on a Jenny Lind bed under an old blue handwoven coverlet made more than a hundred years ago. His night table and chair are Victorian walnut pieces. He made a gun rack to hang on one wall, and he has a roomy closet under the stairway for his clothes and fishing rods.

In the archway between that room and the living room we hung portieres instead of making a door because they take up much less space. When the curtains are drawn back, he gets adequate heat from the oil-burning space heater in the living room.

The third small room became our writing room and is furnished with some of the antiques that came with the house. A walnut grape-carved sofa is upholstered in black leather, tufted. Standing six feet tall is a handmade walnut medicine chest, its two most interesting features being a poison drawer, out of reach of small children, and an upper door of old leaded glass. This glass is red and green, in small rectangles about four by six inches each, and is opaque because of the many bubbles and its thickness. In the top compartment of this case we keep cylinder records for the 1909 Edison phonograph. A mirror-back sidewall whatnot holds art glass of the late nineteenth and early twentieth centuries, and a purple velvet album filled with photographs of our ancestors. On a walnut table are a stereoscope with a box of view cards, a *Godey's Lady's Book* of 1850, and a bound *Puck* magazine of 1889.

Guests who discover this room early in their visit are prone to lose interest in the outdoors. So we don't show it to them nowadays until just before they leave for home—unless we have a rainy day. On such occasions we bring out the stereoscope and the box of view cards and take turns looking at them: the terrible San Francisco earthquake and fire and refugee camps, President McKinley's funeral and grave, and cowboys and Indians of the Old West. We bring out, too, scrapbooks of early greeting cards, old trade cards, and the like, which we keep in the base of the medicine cabinet.

"I'm glad it rained," said one of our friends after a few hours with these items. "In the city we don't take the time to visit our libraries and museums where we could see such things."

"They're more fun to look at in a farmhouse like this," said another.

The floor of the entire downstairs is covered with inlaid linoleum in a marbleized pattern, which unifies the rooms despite the difference in wall colors, and it reduces my housekeeping to a minimum. Henry rented a sander, and he and Walter Kapp sanded the floors and laid the linoleum.

For the narrow stairs I cut inch-wide woolen strips and sewed them together. A Wautoma woman, Mrs. Wilfred Schultz, wove them into a carpet seven yards long.

In the two upstairs bedrooms we placed our hand-hooked and hand-braided rugs, which I had made in the 1930's when we lived on the campus at Mississippi State University.

The open stairwell was a hazard that Henry corrected by

building a hip-high railing along the top, using some of the lumber saved from the century-old white pine tree that was killed by lightning just before we bought the farm.

Where we had to replace ceilings, we used four-by-eight panels of Sheetrock.

"But how will we handle them?" I asked. They were too heavy for the two of us.

"I'll make a T of two-by-fours to hold up one end of the panel," said Henry, "and I'll raise the other end on a ladder. Then after they are nailed in place, I'll tape and lightly plaster the joints. Then it will be your turn. You'll paint the whole thing."

Henry's closet was the only one in the entire house. The attic could be used for some storage, but we found it impossible to mouseproof. So Henry built another closet in what we now call the red room. He made wide shelves at the back of it to hold bed linen.

Downstairs the only walls that needed repair were behind the range and the space heater, where wood had been stacked. I went to Albert Schliepp, the junk dealer in Coloma.

"Albert, how do you mix plaster?" I asked him after borrowing his trowel.

"Well, ain't nothin' to it. You use a stoneware bowl to mix it with water, and then you slosh it on. Only one thing to remember. You gotta have the old edges wet before you put on the new. If you don't have it wet, the new plaster will turn loose atter it dries."

"Plastering is fun," I said to Henry as I slapped it on the wall and smoothed it with the wide trowel.

"I can take it or leave it," he said. But he did daub it on the stair wall where Fritz and I had torn out hunks of old plaster to get rid of the creosote.

The only remodeling was done in the kitchen. By removing walls, Henry made one large cheerful room out of what had been four separate units: a useless back porch, a pantry with open shelves, a wood room, and the dim kitchen with its eight doors and only one window. My cooking area is now where the two small rooms were and is partially cut off from the rest of the room by the sink peninsula, which extends to make a counter alongside the dining space. Without taking a step, I can clear the table and stack the dishes for washing.

The walls of the kitchen are white, and all the furniture is black or white except the one red Boston rocker. A red bandanna cloth on the dining table emphasizes the window and door valances and the chair cushions made of bandanna handkerchiefs. For draw curtains I use white sheeting. It is thick enough to discourage spying while we are absent, and when it is drawn back against the wall, it is inconspicuous.

We consider the kitchen our most successful room. It is surely the most used one. Sometimes while I prepare food, family and guests gather at the dining table to watch wildlife on the terrace. We keep binoculars on the table, for rare is the mealtime when one of us doesn't call the attention of the others to an animal or bird outside. A heron or a white crane may visit the pool bank, or perhaps a once-in-a-season event will occur, such as when fifty or more nighthawks swoop over the meadow, circle madly while catching insects, dip and swirl so fast that all we can determine is that they are large and dark with short tails and long narrow wings. On the underside of each wing is a conspicuous white spot or bar. When flying, nighthawks are hard to follow with glasses, and if we step outdoors they fly away. So we sit indoors and watch their grace and exuberance.

When Henry was ready to remove the rear-porch wall in order to incorporate the porch with the enlarged kitchen, he was able to hire Danny King to help him. Danny was a man of several trades, among them carpentry; his preferred occupation, though, was that of horticulture, which he practiced in a small greenhouse behind his garage in Coloma. He was a capable young man, but we never knew whether he would come when he said he would. If the day was nice, he would decide to work at an outdoor job. Fortunately for us, the weather was windy and cold at the time of Henry's need of him for this particular job. So he came for four or five days.

Once the wall was out, Henry stood back and considered the opening. Where the porch ceiling and the kitchen ceiling joined there was a difference in height of about two feet.

"Would you like a plate shelf up there?" Henry asked me.

"Would I!" A plate shelf would be twenty-two feet long, and I could picture it displaying my old flow-blue Staffordshire plates and pitchers. I hugged him. "You bet I would!"

Danny and he decided to strengthen the structure by bolting two two-by-twelves to the attic wall above where the porch wall had been. Later Henry, worried about a possible sagging of the ceiling despite the supports, set up a two-inch jack post at the corner of the sink peninsula. Painted white, the post is not conspicuous, and Henry's mind is at rest about this specific problem.

To facilitate the flow of heat from the living room to the larger kitchen, he cut a transom above the door and removed the door entirely. Also he cut a hole and inserted a grate on the stair wall just above the furnace to allow heat to go into the red room upstairs. This room had not been heated in any way before.

"Don't do anything to the blue room," I told him. "My room is warm enough. The adjustable grate around the exposed stovepipe gives me enough heat."

My room has the chimney-cupboard type of construction, which was new to me, though I have since found it a common way of building in this region. The brick part of a chimney begins about five feet from the floor of an upstairs room, goes through the attic, and extends above the roof for some three to five feet. The bricks rest on a cupboard of two-inch boards as wide as the chimney itself. As the heat from the exposed pipe coming from the furnace in the room below is never so hot that it warps or scorches items in the cupboard, I can safely keep books there, and bric-a-brac. Even in zero weather, or below, my room heats to a comfortable temperature within a few hours after our arrival.

"For years," I said to Virginia, "I have wasted sympathy on children who had to study and sleep in 'unheated' upstairs rooms. Now I see that they were just as comfortable as their parents were downstairs."

Since pioneer women papered their bedrooms whenever paper was available, I decided to paper mine. Nearly all farm women do the work themselves, and since learning how to do unfamiliar jobs was part of our aim, I asked Laura Rux to show me how to hang paper.

"Papering ain't too hard," she said while she was laying many thicknesses of newspapers on the floor so the wallpaper would remain clean. "It's easy if two people work at it at the same time."

"I'm ignorant but willing," I said.

She placed her two brushes at hand, one for applying paste and one for smoothing out the wrinkles. And she asked me to bring a moist cloth for wiping off excess paste that might ooze out between panels or at the baseboard. She trimmed the left edge of the paper, unrolling and rerolling it as she worked. Then she measured the length of the wall to be covered and added one and a half inches.

"For lapping," she explained. "Ten pieces," she said to herself as she cut ten lengths, the number required for the first wall. Five of these she laid upside down on the news-papers; then she thoroughly spread paste on the back of the top piece, careful to touch every inch of the edge.

"Now hang this piece to the first space in the left-hand corner," she said as she did it, standing on a short stepladder. "We got to get this left edge straight. Oh, oh!" She quickly peeled off the paper and replaced it gently. "There was a bad wrinkle I couldn't 've got out with a brush." She made sure the top was straight too; then she spread the paper down and to the right, first with her hand and then with the shallow brush.

I pasted the second piece and handed it to her. Together we lapped the trimmed edge of this new piece over the untrimmed edge of the first and matched the pattern, which was a small wreath of pink roses on a blue background.

"It's a good pattern," Laura commented, "for if you haven't papered before, it's best to choose a small pattern, not a plain."

"Why?"

"With a plain, the edges that lap over show more."

As soon as each new piece was smoothed into place, we quickly cut off the part left over at the top, if any, with a sharp knife.

Soon I realized I had bought too little paper.

"A single roll doesn't go far, does it?" I observed in dismay.

"Nope. Covers just one yard if your ceiling's eight feet high. Double roll covers a six-by-eight-foot space if you haven't got a door or a window in it."

I later bought some solid-color textured paper to use on the lower vertical part of the wall, using the patterned paper on only the sloping part. That selection was not by choice but by necessity since the other was no longer available. I was alone the day I used the plain blue, and I found that Laura's statement about the overlapping was true; each overlapped edge looked like an inch-wide vertical stripe. However, the overall effect is not a bad one because the regularity of the stripe keeps it from being obtrusive.

For this blue room I refinished some Victorian walnut furniture. Hanging on a towel rack above the washstand are some linen towels of the Civil War period (from my grandmother's trousseau), the kind with woven red bands and long white fringe. Beneath them is a blue and white bowl-and-pitcher set.

For the red room I painted white the old iron bed and the New Goodrich treadle sewing machine.

On the chalk-white stair wall is an exhibit of old handwork: crochet, knitting, tatting, handmade laces, hemstitching, featherstitching, and netting. The collection numbers one hundred and fifty pieces, mostly made by my grandmother, Nancy Clementine Lacey Roquemore, and Henry's mother, Clara Ebner Pochmann. I appliquéd the handwork on red denim and painted all the frames black.

I have been surprised at the interest shown by men who see this display.

"They look like Bohrod's 'magic realism,'" said one.

"I always liked to see a woman doing embroidery," said another.

"My mother had crochet on everything from the top of the piano to the thunder bucket!" declared Emil Schultz. "It was right nice too."

We needed a closet for our many pairs of boots and galoshes. Kay White suggested we build it in the kitchen between the doors to the living room and the stairs, but I liked the spaciousness of the room as it was, and I liked the view from the living room of its twenty-eight-foot length. So I came up with another idea, and Henry made it an actuality.

He took apart an old oak kitchen cabinet (which we didn't need after he enclosed the pantry shelves with doors); the base with its three-by-four-foot porcelain surface became a handy counter between the refrigerator and the gas range. In it we store our cookout utensils. The original top part became a boots cabinet and is convenient beside the door to the entrance porch, an entirely adequate substitute for a closet. Both base and top are painted satin black, like one of the Boston rockers. The big wooden kraut bowl and a smaller salad bowl, together with a butter paddle and a slender tole tray, hang on the white wall above the boots cabinet.

The basement was under only the two-story part of the house. When digging and drilling through the stone walls, Henry discovered they were two feet thick. He went through once to put an outside faucet on the rear terrace. The second time he led a pipe through to the dry well he had dug outside to catch rain water that came in through the entrance. The third time he made a passage for the soil pipe, which leads the sewage into the septic tank.

To make our well, Buschke and Schliepp drove a sand point forty feet down through the ground, attaching one-and-a-quarter-inch pipe sections as needed. Then they installed a jet pump on a concrete platform about six inches higher than the basement floor. The platform, which Henry made, is dished in the center to take off the water when we drain all the pipes, as we do every time we leave after mid-October and up until the first of May.

Used as a potato cellar, this basement originally had wooden partitions. Henry removed them, and now we have good storage space below frost line, which is four and a half feet in Wisconsin.

The last project connected with the house was the building of the twelve-by-fourteen-foot screened porch. On the west side was a door, but there were no steps for it, nor was there a stoop. Perhaps in the mind of the builder there had been a plan to add another room some day, but as far as we could tell, the door had been used for ventilation only.

"That door's in the right place," I said to Henry, "for a porch on that side will get the prevailing southwest breeze and be sheltered by the house from the rains, which usually come from the east. And the views from this side of the house are superb."

We had decided against placing the porch on the rear terrace, though that situation would have made it more convenient to the kitchen. The porch roof, though, would have kept us from enjoying the tall trunks and branches of the white oaks as they arched over the bridge road. We wouldn't have been able to watch the gray squirrels run through their chosen airway while carrying whole ears of golden corn in their mouths. What a ridiculous sight they were—always worth a laugh—for they held one end of the corn in the mouth like a cigar. Nor would we have been able to see the little red squirrel make his dangerous broad jump from the high tip of one oak to an outreaching branch of another on the opposite side of the road. For that leap he started his fast run from the trunk of the first tree, and when he reached the end of that limb his four feet spread out flat to give him leverage as he cleared the eight feet of space between the trees. I always held my breath until he was swinging joyfully in the leaves of the second tree. However, he allowed himself only two arcs before continuing his race along this next lap of his journey to his winter home in a basswood behind the sheds. Several times he built his summer nest in a wren box on the white oak's trunk, enlarging the tiny entrance hole with his sharp teeth.

"I can't believe a squirrel—even a red squirrel—could get into so small a box," said Henry.

"She not only can," I said, "but she can make a nest in there and produce her young. Today four little faces peered out at me!"

Squirrel gender means nothing to me, for both sexes look alike; so I say "he" unless a young one is near, when I can assume the older one is a "she."

Henry wanted to build the porch of our own lumber. Albert Mittelstadt, at his backyard mill in Richford, had sawed our tallest white pine into boards, two-by-fours, four-by-fours, and four-by-sixes, which Henry used in the new part of the kitchen floor and for making the balustrade upstairs.

After cutting many healthy trees threatened by three attacks of oak wilt, he had more logs to be made into lumber.

"A sawyer in Montello will come for a day," Howard Fenske told us, "if he can saw as much as two thousand feet."

So on a hot day in July, Henry and the Fenskes, Eddie Wentland, nephew of the former owner, and George Semrow, a farmer over on County B, took their logs to a designated spot on Cypress Road, and the sawyer brought his portable mill.

It was hard, bruising work for all the men, particularly so for the professor, but he stuck it out, and at the end of the day he proudly brought home in his trailer about seven hundred feet of lumber, which cut considerably the total cost of the new porch.

Henry engaged two carpenters from Springfield Corners, Walter Peschel and Hugo Wruck, to build the frame of the porch and to put on the roof. Henry had first poured concrete foundation posts. Later he laid the floor, made the posts, and spray-painted the underside of the roof. (We had decided not to ceil the porch.) Then I painted the posts and helped him oil the floorboards with raw linseed oil for protection from the weather. Then he put on the copper screening.

The only dirty part of this job was the painting of the underside of the roof. It was impossible to keep the red paint off one's face. Every time Henry climbed down from the ladder, he resembled the devil. I kept turpentine at hand and lots of hot soapy water.

It was a happy day for us when we moved the green glider and red-flowered hammock to the porch. On the warmest days we spend more time there than inside the house, for it catches all the breezes.

One interesting experience for the whole family during the restoration was watching the building of a hornet's nest from the inside of it, so to speak. I found Virginia sitting by a front window in the living room with her neck stretched forward.

"Don't strain yourself," I said, amused.

Without turning her head she lifted a hand to caution me. "It's a bald-faced hornet," she said in a low, excited voice. "The queen is beginning her nest."

On the outside of the windowpane was an inch-wide object that looked like gray cardboard. It had a tiny cavity in its center and a row of "incubator cells" around it. The hornet crawled on top of the cells, in which were tiny white larvae. She paused for two seconds at each cell to feed the larva, which, as soon as it was touched, began to pulsate and continued this pulsation for about eight seconds after the queen had fed it with one swift downward thrust of her head.

As soon as she had made her rounds, she left the nest through the hole in the bottom to search for food. In a few minutes she returned and went through the whole procedure as before but in the opposite direction, clockwise one time, counterclockwise the next. I suppose that arrangement made sure none would be neglected through a possible shortage of food at the end of the bread line.

Henry and I became as interested as Virginia in watching the growth of this nest and its inhabitants. From outdoors the nest looked like a solid globe with a small hole in the bottom, but from indoors, where we were, it was a complex house, and we had ringside seats for the show.

When the first larvae hatched into insects, they crawled around the now crowded nest for perhaps five minutes to dry their wings. Then one by one they left through the hole, returning soon to construct other cells around the outside of their own. From their mouths they exuded a gray substance and, with their front legs, worked it into the shape of a corridor one-fourth of an inch wide, with cells a fourth of an inch square opening off it.

The next morning the new story was complete.

"Why, they must have worked all night!" I said.

"I wonder whether the queen has laid eggs again in the first row," said Virginia, peering close. She could see nothing this day, but a few days later all the cells were full of pulsating larvae and the first workers began taking turns at building and feeding. A second batch of workers hatched, and the indoor activity grew apace. Each worker seemed to be responsible for only three larvae; over these three he crawled, doubling back three or four times to make sure he had missed none. Then he went downstairs to the newest part of the construction and set to work exuding, attaching, and shaping more house. His three larvae were fed again by another worker while the first one was busy building.

In a little while, perhaps eight or ten minutes, the first worker left, and I presume he was the one that came in five minutes later to feed the same three larvae.

"Isn't it fascinating?" Virginia pulled her eyes away long enough to read a little about hornets in three books she had in her lap. She slapped shut one of the books. "That author was just guessing about things, I think. He probably didn't have the opportunity I'm having to see hornets actually doing their work and feeding their young."

"Maybe he had some tame ones in a glass box," I suggested.

"Tame hornets?" She laughed at the idea. "But maybe so. He could have had a queen in a box, and when she had built a little of her nest, he could have let her out to search for her food in the wilds. She probably would have returned just as ours does."

When the nest had grown to the size of a man's fist, Henry began to talk of tearing it down. "I'm almost ready to make the screens for those windows," he reminded Virginia, "and I don't aim to enclose a nest of hornets. That's one thing I don't need, not with another nest of the critters in the attic above my workshop."

Knowing the building of the windowpane nest might go on for another month and therefore delay the restoration of the farmhouse, I nodded agreement.

"There are ten stories now," said Virginia, "and about one hundred and fifty cells, with a new larva in each cell. If you're going to destroy it, you'd better do it now before they hatch."

Henry armed himself with a DDT gun and walked out of the house, with me calling frantically, "Protect yourself with something over your head! Put on a heavy jacket! They'll *kill* you!" I am so allergic to the sting of a hornet, wasp, or bee that I was sincerely frightened for him. But he walked straight up to the window, placed the gun in the hole of the nest, and squirted.

Virginia and I, speechless as we stared through the window, saw every worker and every larva die within a few seconds. Then Henry hurried back to us to avoid the returning workers, which surely would have attacked him when they discovered the calamity.

In September we had to return to Madison for the opening of the University fall term. Before we left Triple Ridge, though the first of September is not the best time for transplanting, I did remove from the woods about a dozen rather large cranberry shrubs to put around the new porch. (I have faith in the success of transplanting at almost any time of the year if the plant is kept wet for several days and moist for some time afterward.) I kept them wet for a few days before we left, and Darrell Fenske continued to water them for another two weeks to insure their survival.

## IV  *Green Clothes for the Naked Hills*

I WISH everybody in the world could plant a tree. The pleasure lasts as long as the tree lives or as long as the planter does. Even though the tree be only a seedling three inches high, setting it out gives satisfaction. It's like creating a piece of the future, something you know will add beauty to the world.

Wanting to do what was right for our land, we took the advice of people who knew, the men who were district managers of soil conservation, watershed management, and wildlife ecology. Whenever there was a conflict in their recommendations, Henry and I made up our own minds, but for the most part we followed, especially in the beginning, their suggestions about where and what to plant on our denuded hillsides, under the scrub oak in woodlands, and in the moist sections of meadow and streamside.

Mr. James Schwoegler was soil manager at the time. He came from Wautoma to walk over the hills with us.

"Problems in woodland and soil conservation," he told us, "often have analogy to those in human illness. Two people may have the same disease, but the doctor prescribes for each one individually, according to his age, his condition, and his medical history. In conservation various situations may present the same problem, but the recommended management program should be tailored to the specific situation."

Henry and I had previously studied the excellent booklet *How To Succeed with Forest Plantations*, put out by the extension service of the University of Wisconsin; hence we were able to understand these specialists as they explained why certain species of trees and shrubs should go in this place or that.

"I'd plant a windbreak along that field edge," Schwoegler told us, pointing to the west fence toward Warrens' farm. "This sandy region is subject to fierce windstorms that blow the light topsoil away. Plant four rows of red pine (Norway) eight feet apart, and six feet apart in the rows."

For the steep side of Pine Ridge he advised alternate plantings: six rows of red, then two rows of white, the rows to be five feet apart and the seedlings six feet apart. When we came to a hillside of scrub oak, he said white pine would do better on the lower moist part and red pine on the higher, drier part.

"This planting will do a lot for your soil." He was enthusiastic. "The pine drops its needles—that is, some of them—while keeping enough to make it look green at all times; the discarded needles make humus and duff, forming a porous sponge to hold water. It's bound to improve your soil for larger timber crops because it raises the water level and increases the flow of springs."

Henry had often in recent months spoken anxiously of the drying up of many small lakes between Endeavor and Coloma. He asked Schwoegler whether the planting of trees had been encouraged in that area.

"Yes, yes. We've held meetings all over in an attempt to get owners to do what you're going to do. With the prevalent draining of marshland around Endeavor and Montello, concentrated plantings of trees and shrubs are a necessity to counteract the damage."

The wildlife manager, Norbert Damaske, agreed that planting would result in more water. "And more wildlife," he said. "Few ducks and geese use a drained marsh."

Henry and I studied our varied terrain after the men left. We wanted to put in as many pines as the plats unsuited to farming would take, but he wanted to save some brushy land for ruffed grouse and quail habitat, and I wanted wild flowers. Virginia wanted open pasture for Trig. So we chose our areas carefully, and then we followed closely Schwoegler's and Damaske's advice as to kind and number of trees and shrubs to plant.

Planting Day was designated each year as soon as we found out when the University's spring vacation would be and when the state nursery at Wisconsin Rapids would have seedlings ready for pickup. They were delivered by truck to Coloma on a weekday, and farmers promptly picked up theirs; but in our case plants might have to remain packaged and in the sun for several days since we could not arrive until Friday afternoon. So we asked permission to get ours at the nursery on a weekend in April.

Planting Day was always an exciting time. In the cabin we arose at dawn and ate a hearty breakfast of poached eggs and broiled patties of venison and pork (frozen during deer season the previous November). That first year Howard Fravel came in time for breakfast and went with Henry to the Rapids, forty miles northwest of us.

While they were gone, Virginia attended to Trig, and I prepared something for lunch that could be heated hurriedly or left simmering for many hours on the wood-burning range in the farmhouse. That day it was a vegetable-and-meat soup, but on other planting days it was sometimes ham hocks and string beans, or spareribs and baked yams—always something that would warm the chilled body and give it strength for bracing the wind in the afternoon. April is a cold month, though usually not snowy.

We welcomed the returning men and exclaimed over the cargo. As long as we had the Packard, Henry used it for this mission; it could hold fourteen thousand pines in bundles of twenty-five seedlings each.

"Unload here," commanded Henry when we reached the farm and stopped beside the yard pump. "Untie the bundles and wet the sphagnum moss covering the roots."

The night before the three of us had filled tubs, milk cans, and buckets with water, each half full as it sat in the trailer attached to the tractor. Now we poked fifty or more seedlings into each container, making sure the tender roots were under water.

"Put about fifty bundles in the trailer," Henry told us. "We should be able to plant that many during the morning. Three thousand a day, Howard said. Didn't you, boy?"

"Yah. With four men working at it, though, and a machine, too, we oughter get in more'n that."

"Well, I should hope so!" wailed Virginia. "We've got fourteen thousand and only two days to plant them!"

"Those as don't get put in," said Howard, "can be heeled in. They'll last long that way. They'll keep, heeled in, till the candles get right long." He held his two hands about six inches apart.

I glanced at the plants on the tarpaulin near the pump. The light-green candles on the white pines were only one-half inch long; the round reddish sprouts on the red pines were smaller than marbles.

Damaske and his helper, Jones, arrived shortly, and on the planting machine that we had rented from the county they left at once for the plat previously selected for the day's work. Henry followed them in his tractor, pulling the trailer filled with pines. Howard, Virginia, and I trudged along happily behind, out of reach of the splashing.

The county machine consisted of two parts. Jones drove the front end, which pulled a flat contrivance on which Damaske sat and fed seedlings into a slot. Each plant fell upright into a shallow furrow made by the machine, and its roots were promptly covered by soil.

Damaske had to be kept supplied with fresh plants. That was Henry's and Howard's job. Virginia and I untangled the roots so that only one pine would be picked up at a time. She and I wore rubber gloves so our hands would not get wet; nevertheless, we often had to stop work to warm our fingers on the hand-warmer Henry had given us. Otherwise we were comfortable enough, for we wore snow boots and snowsuits with fur-lined parkas such as we were accustomed to wearing in the dead of winter. April winds are penetrating, and the noon temperature in mid-April is often cold, in the high twenties or low thirties.

Once that first morning I saw Howard glance at the western sky. I had noticed it was blanketed with gray.

"I hope we get through before it rains," I said to him.

"Rain's the best thing that could happen," he said. "If these trees don't get water in a couple of days, they'll die. They're standing in dry sand."

Damaske had apparently been thinking the same thought, for he suggested we go to lower ground for the rest of the planting that day. Too, he had fallen off the planter twice, the slope was so steep.

"I'd hate to see you on a roller coaster," Henry kidded him.

As we reached a more level area on Middle Ridge, Henry said to me, "Looks like we'll have to plant the hills by hand. They're just too steep for a machine. I'll try to put this first order on the level places. By next season I'll figure out how to get the slopes planted."

At eleven o'clock I left the group and returned to the house to prepare the meal. When I rang the dinner bell, a hungry gang came plunging down the hill. They ate so heartily they didn't seem to notice the stacks of lumber standing about the warm, unfinished kitchen.

Virginia had had enough of the planting, but the men returned to their task. About midafternoon the rain came, a slow, gentle one. In the meantime Virginia and I had dug a shallow trench north of the barn, according to instructions from Damaske. We laid four bundles of separated seedlings so that their roots were in the trench and their green tops on the ground outside. We wet the roots and covered them with soil. A trench one foot deep and three feet long holds a hundred seedlings if they are not more than six inches tall above the roots. Usually the roots are twice as long as the tops. A few had grown eighteen inches tall; we made sure they were put in first so their longer roots would have the needed room.

As the men put their machine and Henry's tractor under the shed, Damaske assured Henry, "You won't lose one of those we put in today. The plants are fresh and moist, and now the rain. Pray for the same sort of conditions every April."

He and Jones waited around a little while; then, deciding the rain was to last a long time, they went home. The next day being a Sunday, the men would not return until the next weekend.

Howard came into the kitchen with us.

"Damaske put three spuds in your workshop," he told Henry. "I'll come help you tomorrow. We can put in a thousand easy."

Henry and he explained the spud method to Virginia and me. One man sank the spud (a long, narrow spade, heavier than the ordinary spade) in the sand and leaned forward, opening a wedge. The second man dropped one of the seedlings into the opening, taking care the taproot was straight down and the laterals not tangled. The third man, with another spud, dropped it an inch or so behind the opening and leaned forward, closing the hole. Then he stepped on the fresh opening with his heel, which left a rounded depression to catch rain water. It was a rapid and easy method of hand-planting where the turf was not thick. We decided that the two women would alternate at handling the plants, but when we tried it we found that the constant stooping tired us too quickly. So the four of us alternated in all three positions.

It was entirely pleasurable after the wind died down about

midmorning on Sunday, and our total for the day was twenty-five hundred. With the thirty-five hundred put in the day before, we had planted six thousand. That left eight thousand to be heeled in.

When the time came for us to leave for Madison, we stood for a moment looking at the space north of the barn.

"It looks like a little cemetery," said Virginia, with a catch in her voice.

It did indeed. The trenches were parallel and varied in length from three to six feet, and were decorated with the green tops of eight thousand seedlings.

The next weekend was a repetition of the first except that the total planted was eight thousand. We were very much pleased with ourselves in this new endeavor, and I was particularly happy over the aid Howard had given us. We sat on the steps, he and I, waiting for Virginia's return from a brief canter on Trig and for Henry's trip to the dog's pen, his signal that he was ready to leave for home.

"Thank you again, Howard," I said to this boy who knew so much about the practical phases of farm life.

He gave me his wistful smile and said, "I like working for Henry. A fellow knows he's going to get paid. Not like some folks I know. I wait and wait and don't have a cent for Sundays."

"But you've been giving us your Sundays."

"That won't last long, though. You don't plant after April."

The planting of the shrubs for wildlife followed the pine planting each year, but after the first two seasons we did not require hired help. Henry hit upon the plan of using his own tractor to pull his trailer of material to the site, unhitching it, and going back to the sheds for his plow. He ran a half-dozen furrows in the grassy spots, then joined Virginia and me, and a possible boy or girl friend of Virginia's from

Madison, to plant the furrows he had just made, which ran crosswise of the slopes and were extremely effective in holding water for the young trees and shrubs.

The tractor did not capsize as had the county planter, but I often held my breath as Henry negotiated a slope or a bog that seemed to me to be dangerous. Howard, on the heavier and more powerful tractor used on Deer Run Farms (the name Sawin had given to the five farms he had bought), came several times to pull Henry out of bogs into which he had driven while planting the wildlife material.

One day after one of these incidents Howard came into the kitchen for a drink of water. He looked concerned.

"Some day you are going to come ask me to pull Henry's tractor off *him* if he don't stop driving up hills too steep and into wet bogs."

I repeated his statement to Henry when he came in for supper. He said nothing, but in the future he used better judgment, for he respected Howard's opinion.

Howard was ready to tell me each Friday of the flowers that had opened in the meadow and woods. He brought me an armful of shad branches one April day.

"This Juneberry's about all that's blooming this month," he said shyly. " 'Course there's windflower up in the hills, but they don't bloom so good if you pick 'em.

"The bluebirds have been here more'n a month, I guess. Starlings have fought 'em pretty bad and taken some of their nests, but there are still some around."

He didn't talk when he was working unless I asked questions. This I did; he had a keen appreciation for wild things, and I was learning from him.

Sometimes during the April planting I took time out to enjoy what we already had—the maples particularly. Both silver and red maples grew at the base of Big Ridge on the north side, and I was attracted by their tiny brushlike blossoms and their two-winged seeds, called keys. I showed them to Virginia. She withdrew her magnifying glass from her pocket and showed me the delicate veining in the translucent wings, and she pointed out the difference in color between the seeds of the silver, or soft maple, which are greenish-yellow, and those of the red maple, which are red. One tall red maple leans against the hill at the widest curve of the stream. I lie beneath it on a sunny day and absorb its scarlet beauty against the blue, blue sky. Thought of this breath-taking sight bolsters me in the winter when the temperature drops below zero.

The maples and paper birches have done a good job of clothing the bare places along Big Ridge. In fact, Henry and I have had to cut some of them in order to keep a wide path for the tractor. Halfway up the side of the ridge, huckleberry patches hold the soil and furnish food for the birds. During our first years at the farm I gathered the huckleberries and made purée of them, but soon I decided they were too much trouble with their large stones (made up of ten parts). Blueberries were much easier to use and to eat. So in recent years I have concentrated on them and the red and black raspberries, dewberries, cherries, and blackberries—all of which grow wild and delicious on hill and in meadow.

Wild grape and crab apple, black haw, plum, and strawberries are other edible native plants that have increased nicely.

Few sugar maples, or hard maples, were left for us. The former owner cut them for firewood, since this maple doesn't throw out sparks as it burns, and it makes clean white ashes. Its flame is steady and cheerful and very pretty with its varying hues. The Wentlands had tapped those trees for the rising sap each February and boiled it down in a three-legged iron pot until it was in syrup or sugar form. I, too, had thought I would try to make a little of that renowned Wisconsin maple syrup, but when I found only three trees large enough for tapping (ten inches) and heard that several dozen gallons of sap were needed to make one gallon of syrup, I gave up the idea. Also, our spring vacation came too late for me to tap the trees at the right time. The pipes which catch the sap must be driven into the tree about four feet from the ground as early as February, certainly no later than early March. The freezing nights and the warm sun of the days can be counted on to cause the wood to contract with the cold and to expand with the warmth, becoming a pump to expel the sap into the pipe, thence into the wooden bucket. The bucket is carried to the kitchen and its contents poured into the big pot on the wood-burning range, where the sap boils for hours and hours, enveloping the whole house and yard with a delectable fragrance.

I was romancing just recently about that old-time custom, but I was rudely brought up by a remark from Henry.

"Most sugarbush farmers now use only plastic tubes," he said. "Plastic buckets and miles of plastic tubing are run from trees to the syrup mill on the big farms. Hundreds of gallons are made instead of a dozen. The early farmers couldn't count on even a dozen gallons of syrup unless they had an extensive maple woodland. I doubt the Wentlands ever made more than five gallons in the best years."

He is probably right. If I were to try it, though, I'd use a wooden pipe and a wooden bucket, for only the old-fashioned method would give me what I want, the delicate smell the pure sap has, the sight and sound of the drop-

drop-drop of the tree's lifeblood into the bucket, fragrant itself of clean wood, and the feeling of satisfaction and expectancy I would have as I detached the full bucket and carried it to my kitchen to cook the sap down.

In 1964 we planted a hundred sugar-maple seedlings among the oaks on the north side of each ridge. We won't live to draw sap from them, but perhaps our grandchildren will.

Another maple is on our land, but I don't search it out or sit beneath it. The ash-leaved maple, or box elder, has no spicy fragrance like the red, and it has no bright autumn gold and apricot color like the others. When its withelike limbs sprout their unmaplelike leaves, an inquisitive bug crawls over them and drops on anybody who sits in the cool shade below. I find it a tree that is attractive to sketch because it is irregular, gnarled, even grotesque sometimes. But the box elder, like the willows, is a litter tree, dropping its brittle branches in every storm.

Along with the sugar maples we planted on the hills we put as many white ash. The ash is a good tree, quiet in form and color, and each of its parts is a thing of beauty if studied separately. Rutherford Platt thinks the white ash should have first prize in tree architecture, for the trunk is straight and tall, giving strength to the tree form. At pine-planting time I often stop at an ash to feel the swelling buds of brown suede and to smile at the funny face inherent in each bud. A few weeks later the multiple leaves dispel the faces, and a month afterward exquisite single-winged seeds grace the limbs.

Both the ash and the sugar maple are assurance to us that our hillsides will have trees, should oak wilt kill the black and red oak now here. Three times the wilt has struck us.

After the first experience, which cost us seven fine trees, Henry bought a power saw, and now when we see a wilted branch in late June or July, we take a twig to the forester. If his diagnosis is wilt, Henry saws the tree trunk as near to the ground as he can. When it crashes to the forest floor, he lops off the limbs to burn, and I sprinkle the stump with Ammate powder, which melts in the sap and soaks into the stump and down into the roots, killing the wilt fungus. We then carefully watch the surrounding trees; if one of them shows a wilted branch, it receives the same sad treatment.

Research on this disease is going on at a rapid pace, and the method of treatment changes from year to year. In 1960 the recommended method involved burning foliage and branches and debarking the trunk if one wished to use the log for saw lumber.

"And the worst of it is," said Henry, "all other oaks in a radius of twenty-five feet of the infected tree have to be cut regardless of how healthy they look."

"Or, if you prefer," said Henry Hill, who had experienced the same sort of attack on his woods farther downstream, "you can ring those surrounding trees with holes drilled in close to the ground, and then you pour in liquid Ammate. If a tree is already infected in its roots, it will show a wilted limb within a few days. Then you cut that one and not the others."

That was a conversation I overheard after our first attack. The second time we lost nine trees, the third time, fourteen. In print that statement is cold fact, but each time a big tree crashed, I wept.

Then, after losing those thirty big trees, we were told that white oak was not so susceptible as the others and that we need not cut the white oak standing near an infected tree!

About half of those destroyed had been of the white variety. Nowadays I occasionally transplant a white-oak seedling to a stand of red or black, just in case.

When Henry and I were searching for land to buy, he often pointed to a grove of white oaks, saying, "Those oaks like good soil, and they put down deep roots. Wherever you see white oak you are likely to find the soil is good."

So I learned to recognize its characteristics. The bark is close-knit and lighter in color than that on the other oaks, almost pearly gray at times, and the leaves have rounded lobes and valleys, like the dips between the fingers of my hand and like the leaves of sugar maple.

"Notice the sun falls through this oak," said Henry, "but the shade under a black oak is as dense as that cast by a wall."

It is true. The sunlight makes filigree shadows beneath a white oak.

The acorn is smooth and lighter in color than the fruit of oaks in the other family, the Black Oak Group. Its cap covers only about a third of the nut. It matures and falls and disintegrates within one season, so squirrels eat these acorns when found, or soon after, not depending on them to last through the winter. When I gather them for making bunches of "grapes" for winter arrangements, I get them early in the morning before the squirrels, jays, and field mice can eat them; then I roast them at a low heat for an hour to kill any worms that might be inside them.

"Indians and pioneers often ate roasted acorns," Henry reminds me.

"But only in time of great need. Didn't they usually feed them to the hogs?"

"They still do, I guess. Lots of nourishment in acorns."

"We'll never starve then."

Another tree of the White Oak Group is the great bur oak. Our burs are scattered through the lowland among black cherries and cottonwood. In time these lesser trees will give way to this magnificent patriarchal tree, which, when mature, will allow no understory growth except long prairie grasses.

"That's a long time off," said Henry. "Ours are not more than ten to twelve inches in diameter. Bur oaks grow big horizontal limbs and massive trunks. I know one down on the Mecan that must be six or seven feet in circumference."

"Oh? Better tell Walter Scott about it."

"Who's he?"

"He's the man who collects information about the largest trees in the state, and he finds out whether the Wisconsin trees hold the national records for size. I think it's a hobby with him." From my hip pocket I drew a measuring tape. "See? I nearly always carry one of these with me nowadays to measure trees I happen to come across."

Henry looked at me in surprise. "You do manage to get yourself involved, don't you?"

Henry recognizes trees by their form and bark; I usually have to see their leaves also. Though the bark of the bur oak is easily recognizable because of its dark color and its deep ridges, I like to examine the leaves too. Like those of other members of the White Oak Group, the bur-oak leaf has rounded lobes and valleys, but a bit below the middle is a deep cut, where the opposite sinuses almost meet at the central vein. This is a distinguishing mark. The bur-oak acorn is covered almost entirely by its deep shaggy cup, and because of it the tree is sometimes called the mossy-cup oak.

John Muir, Wisconsin's most famous naturalist, now called "the father of the national forest," lived among bur-oak openings about twenty miles south of Triple Ridge Farm. He made a study of this longevous and fire-resistant tree. The "openings" were so called because, since only grass carpeted the area beneath the trees, a man could see a long way.

The term "scrub oak" is loosely applied to small- and medium-sized oaks that run apace up the hillsides and across abandoned fields over much of our nation. Ours belong to the Black Oak Group and are chiefly the varieties called red and black. This black oak should be called yellow oak since it has so many yellow parts: the lining of the acorn cup, the meat of its nut, and the inner bark of the trunk and limbs. (This is tannin, a chemical used for tanning leather.) The red-oak member has a smooth reddish-brown bud and reddish midrib on its leaves, which are oval in shape rather than pearlike as are those of its neighbor. Its leaves are varied, but all oaks have that peculiarity; it is well nigh impossible to find two leaves exactly alike on any member of the species.

The native Wisconsin black willow is the variety along our stream, though a few weeping willows grow where I have stuck in fresh twigs. In winter and early spring the yellow willow branches vie in brightness with the red-twig dogwood shrubs, both loving moist ground.

Next spring we are to plant a hundred black-walnut seedlings. Mr. Wentland, on his first visit to see what we were doing with his old homeplace, pointed to the only walnut tree on the acreage.

"That," he said, "came from walnuts I used to throw to the hogs."

"Does it bear?"

"Yah. But you wont get any nuts."

"Why?" Walnuts rate high with me.

"Squirrels. One day you see big green walnuts. Next day, all gone. Squirrels store dem in trees for winter."

And that's the way it has been. Not one walnut have we had from our tree. The new ones we shall plant will not bear in time to feed us, perhaps, but they will be of use to our descendants because there will be more trees than squirrels!

Red cedar in small colonies is populating the north slopes of Big Ridge and Middle Ridge, and tamarack (larch) is coming into the marsh. Tamarack needles scatter haphazardly up and down the ragged branches, blue-green and tender in summer and bright gold in autumn. They drop off in November, leaving tiny smooth brown cones to delight the eye. Red cedar, on the other hand, retains its needles, which are mostly scales, and against the snow it presents a dark brownish-green pyramidal image. Its blue berries attract cedar waxwings, but I have noticed these birds eat daintily, politely, in unhurried fashion. Could that mean the taste is sort of acrid, like that of the cedar wood?

Among the coniferous trees we watch for the sign of grubs—white gummy substance oozing out of injured bark. An ice pick shoved into the blob can kill the grub, but too often the infected place is far out on a branch that is too weak to hold the weight of a person or even to balance a ladder. If spraying it doesn't help, the tree must be cut and burned to prevent further infection in the plantation. Fortunately, we have had few such infestations.

Porcupines, rabbits, and deer can do a great deal of injury to young plants, but at Triple Ridge we have noticed none to speak of. Field mice seem to have enough food in the meadows; deer eat the white cedar that we put in specifically for them, and they like dogwood. For rubbing off their velvet they have chosen two red cedars a half mile from the house. Porcupines are seldom seen in the Richford area. In some severe winters, when snow remained two feet deep or more around the shrubs and young trees, rabbits nearly ringed them. Crab apples were particularly hard hit on those occasions, but they seem to have remarkable recuperative power so that, unless they are ringed in two or three successive seasons, they heal nicely. We have lost only six out of fifteen hundred crab apple trees.

Blister rust is a threat to white pine if either gooseberries or black currants grow within nine hundred feet; these bushes are hosts to the wind-blown spores of the rust. After losing several trees, we searched for and destroyed the host bushes.

Tip weevil has been our chief pine enemy. It deforms a tree by killing its leader; when another branch has to take over as the head, the trunk has a hump and cannot become a straight saw log. Carrying a shoulder sprayer, Henry walked through all our plantations and sprayed every white pine. It was a wearing task requiring three weekends, but it saved the pines.

Mr. Schwoegler was the first to show us the symptoms of the grub and the tip-weevil damage.

"Get rid of the Scotch pines in the plantation across from your house," he advised. "The Scotch, being an imported tree, is less resistant to disease and spreads the grub and weevil to your better trees."

My nephew, Casey Fouts, of Texas, was a guest at the time. One day he and Henry cut a dozen of the infected trees; then Henry came into the house to rest.

"Are you sure Casey knows how to wield that ax?" I was rather anxious about a fifteen-year-old who had grown up in a city home.

"Seems to. He has only three more to cut." Henry walked into his bedroom just as Casey burst into the kitchen.

"Oh, Ruth! I've knocked down a tree Henry told me not to cut! Come quick!"

The three of us hurried to the injured tree. It was a healthy white pine about ten feet high standing at the edge of the flower border.

"Somehow my ax went the wrong way and cut the wrong tree!" Casey was sorely distressed. "I don't know how it happened."

Henry examined the cut. "I'll tape it," he said calmly. While he went to his workshop, Casey and I set the severed part of the trunk straight on the stump, matching the furrows in the bark as well as we could. The ax had slashed nearly all the way through, leaving only a half-inch of flesh and bark to hold the two parts together.

Henry came back and wrapped his sticky green tape around and around the trunk for a space of about six inches; then he tied a little rope to hold it in place. Today that tree is about twenty feet tall and is a beauty. We call it "Casey's pine."

Casey's twin brother, Court, was a guest in another year. It was he who built for us some short check dams on the narrow, deep trail that Trigger had worn on the side of Big Ridge. Court laid logs across the trail and steadied them by driving stakes near the ends; then he filled in behind them with soil and stones.

"I learned how to make these dams at a Boy Scout camp in New Mexico," he said. He'd be proud of his work if he could see the sites today. Pines that I planted at the ends of his logs now meet in the center, and the soil has stayed in place, allowing a ground cover of false lily of the valley and dayflower to grow down the hill. Bearberry and Virginia creeper, too, have appeared there. Erosion is a danger of the past.

Most tree growers of the state are now shearing their pines before selling them as Christmas trees. We have not yet succumbed to the practice. To us, it seems factitious; the form of the pine, so beautiful in its natural state, should not be tampered with. But as the years have gone by, we have seen that shearing does make the tree more compact, more dense, more solidly pyramidal for use in a room. Perhaps we have missed the boat that brings in the money; however, neither Henry nor Harold Fenske seems eager to make money on the trees.

"Each tree," says Henry, "needs a square rod for final timber growth. We'll have to cut some to save the others, but that time hasn't come. We'll sell those for pulp."

When we spend a Christmas at the farm, we don't use a sheared tree. We choose a symmetrical jack pine, with its dainty short needles and open frame that allows the hanging trinkets to twirl with every breeze; or we use a natural balsam fir that looks like the illustrations in a Kate Greenaway book, or a pine that has grown so slowly its whorls are fairly close together. Spruces lose their needles too quickly. Cedars are satisfactory but not as green as the other conifers at that time of year, and some people are allergic to the needles, breaking out in a rash.

Professional Christmas-tree growers and dealers tell us that a tree will keep its needles longer if it is cut before the first really hard freeze comes and is stored in a cool place until time for its decoration. These people should know, for Waushara County grows more conifers for the festive season than does any other county. Wautoma, the county seat, is now called by its progressive businessmen "The Christmas Tree Capital of the World."

Now when I meditate about this whole venture in re-forestation and in woodland management at Triple Ridge, it seems to me our activity began to pay off immediately in increased beauty and interest. It is truly amazing how interesting baby conifers can be. I had an inner glow every time I walked through our new plantations, particularly in late fall after October color faded from the deciduous trees and shrubs and grasses. The neutral grays and beiges of a hillside were accented by the little dark-green pines, like exclamation points, and the larger pines atop the hills gave emphasis to the line of demarcation between mauve hill and gray-blue sky. Later, when the snow fell and covered the little pines, protecting them from sun-burning, I gloated over the post-card pictures on every hand, each pine branch holding a scrap of fleecy white blanket. The snow at the farm is always chalk-white since no soot is there to begrime it. The contrast, then, of dark green and unsoiled white is startlingly beautiful. Shadows and distance lend a soft blueness. Down by the stream, which flows too fast to freeze, the pines we set into the eroding banks to hold them in place now form a green roof above snow caverns made by the blue water ripples as they lick at the bank.

# V    *Moon in Birch Pond*

"IT JUST might work," mused James Schwoegler as he stood with chin in hand contemplating the moist meadow between the house and stream.

If I had had serious doubts about whether a pool could be dug there, I might have taken that remark to be a negative one, but as I believed the soil would hold water, I interpreted his words as encouraging. Earlier I had dug a hole about a foot deep in the small spring flowage and had found white sand. If the sand formed a layer through the whole of the meadow, my dream pool could become a reality.

Mr. Schwoegler's glance went up the hills and traversed the slopes and came to rest in the meadow around us.

"I'm wondering," he said, "whether your plantings will slow up the runoff so the pool won't be silted in. And I'm wondering, too, whether a pool as small as you are planning, a third of an acre, will hold enough water to help control the usual flooding of the stream during the thaw."

"We'll make the spoil bank on the low side quite high," I promised. The plan was to use the removed soil for the building of the banks; there was to be no dam or outlet. That was the customary way to build small pools in Waushara County.

"I don't want you to dig a big hole here and then find your soil won't hold water. Tell you what: I'll bring the engineer over here and let you know what he says. It just might work."

During the week we had a letter from him saying the engineer was doubtful that the peaty soil would allow us to have a satisfactory pool. In the meantime I had already written to J. P. Szukis of Plainfield, whom Bill Wichner had told me of, and had asked him to come to our farm the next Saturday to determine whether we were wise in planning a pool. Bill had told me Mr. Szukis was an experienced pool digger, with a dragline as well as a bulldozer.

On Friday Henry outlined the proposed shape of the pool by plowing a row through the tough roots of the meadow. I cringed as I watched him. The tractor wheels slipped and slithered over the hummocks. Henry's hands were jerked off the steering wheel, and his head snapped back as though his neck had let go of the spine.

"You're loosening the roots," I called, "but you're loosening your brain tissue as well!"

"No, just my teeth," he answered grimly.

"Wait till Szukis arrives tomorrow. Your work may be in vain."

On Saturday the man came, and he and I walked over the tract. He stopped where I wanted the deep water and he dug a hole with his spade. Three feet down he found white sand, which he raked off his spade. He patted it on his palm.

"O.K.," he said, nodding approval. "This is the kind of sand you need. When it's wet, it hardens. It'll hold water."

"When can you come?" I was ecstatic.

"Well, my summer work's done. Maybe I can come next Thursday."

It was in late September, and the University had already opened. Chances were that Henry would not be able to leave Madison again for two or three weeks.

"Fine," I said. "I'll be here about eight o'clock Thursday morning and I'll expect you."

When Henry returned from his errand in Coloma, I told him of the plan.

"All right. The pool is your project anyway. You know what you want. I won't have to be here."

So I came alone to meet Szukis and his helper. They had arrived earlier and had decided to take the big monster, the dragline machine, down the narrow bridge road behind the house instead of through the meadow by the garden. At the top of the road, when the driver climbed down from his seat—for some unknown reason—the big machine slipped its brake and, plunging recklessly, crashed down the entire length of the road and came to a halt only after the spongy peat moss of the meadow sank enough beneath the tremendous weight to prevent continued progress. Szukis was still sort of shaken when he told me about it.

His helper shook his head. "Don't know why it stood up. It ought to of fell over," he told me.

With trepidation I walked the road to check the damage. As the space alongside was the only cleaned-up area that I was sure would not be trespassed on during the renovation of the house, I had planted there every plant given me by friends and all the nursery stock I had ordered for the perennial border along the driveway. Now this! But I was in for a nice surprise. Nothing but a wild elderberry had been leveled, and a log or two, which I had laid to mark the edge of the road, had been knocked askew. That was all.

That day and half of the next the giant jaws of the machine snapped at the meadow, lifted, and dumped. Earlier in the week a rain had softened the hummocks so that the machinery often tipped precariously. The men laid unwieldy mats of logs and drove the machine up on them, but even so it nearly slipped off several times. Shifting the mats took time and slowed the digging. I began to do some nervous calculating; at thirteen dollars an hour the job was fast eating up my hoarded two hundred and fifty dollars. But when the men left for home with my money, the gaping hole was roughly seventy-five feet by two hundred and seventy, and water was rising rapidly. The "floor" was indeed white, but the peaty "walls" were as black as crow.

"So muddy!" I said to myself as I watched the water seeping down the sides into the deepest end. The depth there would be ten feet, Szukis had said. "Ten feet of mud! How wonderful to dive into."

But my misgivings were short-lived, for pool water, like

love (according to Plutarch), though at first confused, if given time will settle and clarify.

About dinner time I heard Henry's beep-beep and knew that he and Virginia, eager to see what had been done, had come up, though they both had told me they would be too busy in Madison to spend any time at Richford that weekend. Happy and I ran from the kitchen to greet them.

"It's done!" I shouted. "And it's filling up fast."

"How big is it?" This from Virginia.

"Did your money go far enough?" Henry was amused at my excitement.

"Come see!"

In the twilight the spoil banks were mottled black and white and seemed even higher than they actually were.

"Gosh, Mom, he must have dug to China!"

It did look deep. The water appeared black now, and the white sand was covered entirely.

Henry said nothing for a while, just stood with his hands in his pockets and smoked a cigarette.

"It's only a foot deep in the west end," I told them, "but it's ten feet deep in this end; so we can dive if we wish, and fish can live through the winter under the ice—if you want to put fish in, Henry."

"Nope, this is your pool. For swimming and for beauty, you said."

I contemplated the scene in the fading light. "I'm afraid it won't be very beautiful for some time to come, but it will be interesting, won't it?"

And it was. Particularly for Virginia, the pool, pregnant with life, was the most interesting feature of the farm. That year in high school she was planning to enter the Westinghouse Talent Search for young scientists; her project was

the breeding of Siamese fighting fish, for which she had a
private laboratory in our Madison basement. The pool at
the farm, then, became her second lab, offering such quantity and variety of aquatic life that she spent little time
swimming, though she spent hours in the water. She took
*Daphnia* from the pool and fed them to her tropical fish;
then she kept records of the acceleration of activity and the
increased brilliance of color.

"Mom, the pool has more variety of temperature than the
stream has," she explained, "and that's one reason it has such
variety of insects. It's rich water too."

"What do you mean by rich?"

"Well, its new water comes from the surface and from
rain and melted snow. Rain and snow don't have many
minerals, but surface water does. It's rich. Of course, new
water from seepage and from springs, too, comes in; that's
soft water. What I'm trying to say is that our pool has more
minerals than a strictly seepage pond would have. That's
why it has so much life."

I saw that I had much to learn about pools.

Many of our Richford friends came over to watch Henry
work at smoothing the banks. With scraper and scoop he
managed to make a flat surface sufficiently wide for the
tractor in case he ever needed to repair a washout.

"Henry's made a race track around the pool," said Ray
White.

Once four of us—Ray, Howard, Virginia, and I—had to
rush to Henry's aid as the tractor slid down the bank backward. While three of us hung onto the front wheels, Howard
deftly removed a strong rope from where Henry had coiled
it behind his seat and gave it a turn about the rear axle.
Then he and Ray pulled the rope while Henry drove to safe

ground. Howard sighed as he slowly shook his head at me.

Prairie grasses came up on the banks and grew so rank that we did not need to set out other things to hold the soil. The first spring, grasses trailed prettily in the water and sent up handsome ivory plumes as spectacular as the most exotic flowers would have been. The second year meadow flowers came through this soil, exposed for the first time since it was deposited by the glacier more than ten thousand years ago.

"Why, it's as fertile as the best field I've got," said Henry in surprise.

"It's a mixture of peat and sand and crushed glacial rock," I said meditatively, as I admired the dainty pink phlox and Golden Alexander among the grasses. "That soil hasn't seen the light of day or smelled the fragrance of growing things since the days of the dinosaurs."

Cattails, willows, birches, the brilliant butterfly weed, blue vervain, black-eyed Susan, pussy willow—all these and more grew beautifully there, so that nowadays the area is indeed a fulfillment of my desire.

Though Henry was pleased with the way the pool filled and remained full even during July and August, the sight of water without fish eventually proved too much for him.

"I'll see whether I can get a few bass from Wayne Moore at Curtis Lake," he said as he placed a zinc tub in his car trunk. "If not, then I'll ask Damaske whether he can get a few for me."

He came back with four black bass and four bluegills. He and Virginia put them into the water, with Happy watching intently beside them and sniffing the water eagerly after each fish made his splash.

"Dad," said Virginia as the two of them sat on the weathered plank bench that Henry had placed among the hawthorns and gray dogwood at the shallow end, "Dad, I'm not sure it's a good idea to put two different kinds of fish in this pool. The bluegills are more prolific than the bass, and the pool may not be able to feed all that will be produced. They'll be stunted."

"If they survive the winter," added her father. "I don't think they will. Even if they do have enough free water below the two or three feet of ice, they won't have enough oxygen."

"There's a lot of plant life already," said Virginia, "and more will be coming in all the time."

The following May, Virginia shouted to me as I rested in the glider on the rear terrace, "Oh, Mom! Come look! Tens of thousands!"

"Of what?" She was standing in water up to her waist. This was to be her first swim of the year, and she was entering gingerly, not jumping in or diving as was her wont.

"Fry! There are clouds of fry all along the bank about ten feet apart. Come quick!"

I ran down the bridge road but approached her slowly so as not to frighten the young fish. She stood very still.

"Look just in front of you, close to the grass. That school is about a thousand fry!"

I saw the cloudlike mass. "At least two hundred." I couldn't resist trying again to stop her growing habit of exaggeration. "Neither Henry nor I have been able to find any fry at all. You have better eyes than we."

"I'm afraid they're bluegills," she said dubiously, squinting at them and leaning closer.

In October she and her father had dug several trailer loads of white gravel from Elmer Wieland's pit and had put it in the shallows of the west end of our pool, hoping the bass would use it for spawning beds. They, like trout, prefer gravel to sand for such purpose. But apparently the bluegills had appropriated the beds. Henry's motive for placing the old bench near them had been to watch the bass hover over the eggs until they hatched. But spring had come late that year and Henry's chores had been many, so that he had not been able to use the bench often. I had been busy gathering specimens for the University herbarium, so neither of us had noticed the guarding or the hatching. In fact, when we took our first spring reconnaissance walk, only two fish came up to look at us.

"They're so hungry they hope we'll fall in," I commented.

"I didn't think they'd live through the winter," Henry said. "The others probably ate one another."

I considered that. "But the bass would eat the bluegills, wouldn't they? And these we see today are bluegills, aren't they? I can't see a little palm-sized bluegill devouring an arm-sized bass."

And now Virginia had discovered the young.

I walked the banks daily thereafter, throwing oatmeal and bread crumbs to the older fish, of which there seemed to be six; soon they became more tame, and promptly upon my approach they would come up for a handout.

By the third season the bluegills had won. We saw no more bass. The more prolific smaller fish had taken over the premises. We didn't really mind, for we ate neither. Spoiled as we were by having enough of the more delicate trout, we never ate any other kind. Also, the bluegills ate the stinging backswimmers as readily as the bass did.

The backswimmers caused us some trouble. No men were stung in our pool; since they wore only swim shorts, the insect was able to get away. But during the first two seasons Virginia was stung every time she went in. The insect would get caught in her bra and, unable to dive to the bottom of the pool as was his custom when disturbed, he would sting her.

She caught one and brought him indoors so I could see him. In her aquarium he hung head downward from the surface, his ventral side up, and his four short legs held rather close to his body, but his two hindmost legs, fully twice as long as the others, were brought forward and were used like paddles to move him along.

"Strange creature," I said.

Virginia introduced me to many unfamiliar and beautiful things. Sometimes we lay on the stream bank in late spring and watched a minute-old mayfly hover while the rushing water dragged eggs from her egg sac.

"She exists for this one purpose and then dies on the water," Virginia told me.

She pointed out such minutiae as insect eggs beautifully encrusted with intricate shells as they rested on a leaf of water plantain. She explained the difference between dragonflies and damselflies, both of which, God bless 'em, prey on mosquitoes and midges.

"Dragonflies drop their eggs on the surface, but damselflies deposit theirs on the plants in the shallow water, and they'll sit on low plants at the edge of the water for a long time. But dragonflies flit here and there, very fast, and often return to the same piece of eragrostis."

"Of what?"

"Grass."

"Oh."

"Here's a piece." She touched a spikelet with spreading feathery parts.

"I have a lot to learn about grasses," I sighed.

"I still have a lot to learn about cooking," she said, smiling.

I watched a dragonfly, opalescent and swift, settle for a moment on the grass, his finely netted wings held straight out from his body. A few feet away was a damselfly, a brilliant green body with spoon-shaped black wings.

"Are they both called devil's darning needle?" I asked.

"Well, I think locally they are, but the term's usually for the dragonfly, I think. So is the term snake doctor."

From the two hammocks we see much bird life, but the one near the pool between a white oak and the bird bush, as Henry calls the big Tartarian honeysuckle, which always has a nest in it, is the better vantage point. The hammock is only a few feet from the water on the north side and the same distance from a natural bog on the south. The meadow is near, as are the rock wall and flower bed alongside the bridge road, and the Wildwood lies to the west. On the rear terrace is the feeding station. So the hammock is one of the best places on the farm for watching and listening. If I could refrain from slapping at mosquitoes, as can Henry, I'd see and hear more, but even so I have some fine experiences.

One day I saw a catbird courtship there. On a wide horizontal limb stretching out over the bog a female catbird lit. A second later the male came. They stood looking at each other with their heads slightly cocked. The female backed into a leafy twig. The male danced for her. He fluffed his neck feathers and spread his wings; he hopped, stiff-legged, toward her, then away from her, back and forth on the limb, covering about four feet of its length. Twice he leapt upward, facing her still, and repeated his dance each time. Then he lowered his wings, let his feathers fall into place, and sat on the limb in his usual manner as if nothing had happened.

The female stretched herself, flapped her wings two or three times, and then settled back into the leaves. The male went through the whole dance anew. Then she hopped out on the limb to meet him. They seemed to brush against each other before flying abreast to the pool; they drank and winged their happy way toward Birch Pond.

I hoped they would be the pair to build in the bird bush that spring, and perhaps they were.

I closed my eyes and listened. A song sparrow warbled on the stream bank, a farm pigeon cooed urgently from the west end of the pool, where he had probably lit on a slender sand bar, old leaves rustled beneath me as a beetle or a field mouse picked his way among them, a sparrow hawk staccatoed his six high-pitched notes from the tall poplars along the Fenske line, and a phoebe called his name from the area near the shed with the broken window, where he built each April.

One hot dry June the pool became green with algae, unattractive to swimmers. I wondered whether long-dormant nutrients from the glacial soil, and maybe from strata deposited over thousands of years after the melting of the glacier, were far richer than we had suspected. It was an intriguing thought, and I have no answer yet.

We tried several methods of removing the algae. First, Henry and I raked out quantities with leaf rakes, snagging the edge of a green cloud of it and pulling carefully until an amount that seemed to be gallons floated to the bank at our feet. Once lifted out on land, however, it shrank to a few pints. The more we pulled out, the more there seemed to be in the water.

Secondly, we unrolled some chicken wire, put sticks in the ends, and with Henry holding it on the north bank and Virginia and me holding it on the south, we submerged it and walked slowly toward the shallow end, pulling the algae caught in the wire. That would have been a perfect method had we been giants, but Virginia and I quickly gave out. Henry then attached his end to the tractor and pulled it. Virginia and I tried to hold on to our end to prevent its going under water, but we were not of much use, for we were weak with laughter bordering on hysteria when twice we barely saved each other from being drawn into the turbid mess.

Slowly and relentlessly, the tractor dragged the slimy green dragon (the wire had curled and was entirely coated) through the reeds and sedges and left it in the meadow to dry.

The next weekend the algae was as thick as ever!

"Dr. Wisby will know what to do," said Virginia, who by that time was a sophomore at the university and had worked some with Dr. Warren Wisby in an experiment to determine whether fish used sunlight for navigation. She had faith in his ability to accomplish anything pertaining to aquatic life.

It was autumn before she actually asked him for advice.

"It's too late now," he said, "but next April I'll have a look at your pool."

The next April he came, and he did tell us what to do; indeed, he helped do it. Virginia and her new friend, Ted Weis, a junior premed student at U. W., went to Wautoma for twenty pounds of copper sulfate, and Henry got the recommended germicide at Coloma. The three men applied the materials to the surface as evenly as they could throw them. (A calm day must be chosen for this maneuver, or the wind will blow all the powder to one end of the pool.)

That did it. We had no more algae for three years. The fish were not killed and they spawned that season. The water became clear and cool, and Virginia and Ted swam twice a day during their vacation.

Whenever algae appears again, Henry and I sprinkle copper sulfate without the germicide; if we do that before the growth is dense in any one spot, we control the condition.

Though I don't often swim, the pool has been from the beginning a real part of my life at the farm. I drink in its early-morning beauty when the enveloping fog is rising in a sheet, disintegrating slowly into veils and wisps of chiffon, and turning blush-pink at the first kiss of the sun. Soon the white oaks hide the pink plumes from me, but for several minutes I can continue watching their reflection in the water while, as little rosy clouds, they drift eastward.

One of my most memorable sights was in such a setting and at such a time. I had awakened early and walked to the north window upstairs to look on the pool and meadow before dressing. The fog that morning was dense and had not broken up. It had turned pink all through, from ground to treetop. It was a soft fluffy wall, and against that wall, just there below my window, stood a lovely large doe—*looking at me*. I stood very still, and so did she, for perhaps a full minute. Then she quietly backed into the pink stuff and was enveloped by it.

I breathed again. We had stood there looking into each other's eyes, both full of wonder and without fear. That experience filled my reservoir of spiritual energy for the day; indeed, the picture has stayed with me for years.

From the kitchen all of us watch swallows swoop over the water for insects, see the phoebes go to the edge of the water for their little mud "bricks" for house building, the robins for mud to line their nests, and farm pigeons from

Fenskes' and Fravels' and Sawins' to light for but a moment
on the sand bar, where they take one drink and then fly
swiftly away as if frightened within an inch of their opalescent beauty. The killdeer and the plover haunt the shallow
end.

This past summer a song sparrow built his nest on the
bank. We had come to associate this bird with the stream,
for a song-sparrow nest may often be found every fifty feet
or so the length of the creek. We are happy to have these
birds coming nearer the house to raise their young, for they
are among the most welcome birds on the farm. Their
cheery songs and their diligent scratching for insects among
the leaves and plants of the rock garden endear them to us.
They accept us more readily than do most of the other wild
birds, and often they do not fly away when we come out on
the terrace to strew crumbs, barley seed, rye, buckwheat, or
whatever else we happen to have.

Two years ago we decided to have a second pool, this one
to be dug at the base of Big Ridge where a spring already
flowed into the stream; this flowage was everlasting, a guar-
antee that a pool would have fresh water. It meant also that
it should have a dam with an outlet.

I staked the desired shape, like a gourd with the stem of
the gourd crooking around a peninsula and stopping about
fifteen feet from the stream. The dam would be placed
there, and Henry and I would build a waterfall on the lower
side of the dam. This pool, which we later named Birch
Pond, would be purely for beauty and the birds.

"You ain't going to stock it?" Young Ricky Zuehlcke was
incredulous. "It'll be a good place for rainbows."

Ray White agreed. "It'll be a natural for rainbows, Henry."

"Yes," said Henry, "and as soon as word got around, seiners would come in while I'd be in Madison and would take every trout."

So Birch Pond, out of sight of buildings and road, reached by only a path alongside the balsam firs and Trigger's steep course downhill from the corral, is haunted mainly by air creatures such as flycatchers, warblers, Bohemian and cedar waxwings, woodpeckers, and us. On its highest bank, star moss invites close inspection from every visitor; the male plants send up tiny brown spires, and the females sport a globular bloom of bright red about the size of a pinhead—known locally as "British soldiers." In July spikes of purple-fringed orchid march through the fen beyond the pond, and delicate lady's-tresses peek through the grasses. All summer, native forget-me-nots make blue the ground at the edge of the water beneath a "family" of white birches. In August purple *Liatris spicata* lives up to its local name, gayfeather, and lifts my spirit.

Come September, fringed gentian inspires the poet in me. I have counted as many as forty-four blossoms on one gentian plant—that one in the adjoining fen where it was shaded by taller cattails, heavier skunk cabbage, daintier bogbean, and blackberries.

Joe-pye weed, as feathery in reality as in reflection, and lobelia, as red in the water as on the bank—these and more entice me away from the few household duties from the first of May until the last of October. Then, just before the water freezes, the reflections are of the sky and bare trunks, which are as interesting in their way as are the colorful flowers.

Every visit to this pond area turns up something new for me—perhaps a towhee nest low in a cranberry, or an indigo bunting nest on a willow branch overhanging pool or stream, or maybe a nestling dead on the ground where he has fallen from an oriole cradle. Teal and redheads, too, sometimes fly up when I approach; in time they may associate my coming with the food I bring and will remain to be sociable.

Though both pool and pond freeze over, they freeze quite differently. Birch Pond, fed by a spring or multiple springs, has thin ice. We can see where the springs are, for the ice directly above them has gray figurations resembling a tree with many branches. No one would dare try to skate on Birch Pond. The larger pool, though, freezes well, and from about the first of December it is safe for skating. Young people who do not live where pond water freezes will be interested to learn that if the surface has frozen during a snowstorm or a strong wind, it will be very rough, but if it has frozen on a calm day, the surface will be mirror smooth. After each snowfall a hand scraper must be used to push the snow back toward the bank so skaters will have enough room for their racing and dancing and spinning. Nothing is so colorful and gay in a Wisconsin winter as a skating party.

I must confess, though, that I get my fun in watching, not skating; my usual vantage point is the warm kitchen, where I do my bit by keeping a big pot of coffee on the range and a filled doughnut jar on the table, plenty of dry towels at hand, and a variety of mukluks for those who want to doff their shoe skates for a while. Virginia likes to sit in the red Boston rocker with her feet in the oven until she has "warmed from the bottom up," as she says.

When snow has not been removed from the ice, we see many fascinating tracks there. I once sketched them in charcoal on heavy white paper and kept it around until we had identified all of them: field mouse, rabbit, owl, deer, fox, weasel, jay, kingfisher, skunk, quail, ruffed grouse, pheasant, and perhaps a hawk.

As the ice begins to go out in April, the open water is very blue. The beige grass and the luscious pines make a serene reflection unless it is dissolved in the waves made by two frolicking muskrats.

So for all of us and our guests the pond and the pool are two of the most interesting and appealing features of our farm. It is said that work is only play if you enjoy it. So we play around these water holes on each visit, however short.

One slow evening in September, that best of all months in this state, Henry and I strolled lazily down Fir Lane to Birch Pond. We came to it just as a full red moon smiled at us over the treetops to the east. A second moon in the water returned the smile upside down. The red moons darkened the scene with their sudden brightness, and we, standing there holding hands like younger lovers, were full-hearted with enchantment and a sense of our good fortune.

# VI *Wildlife Habitat*

F R O M the first spring of our ownership, when Damaske
and Jones began the planting of pines and shrubs to help
the wildlife, this project intrigued all three of us. Each of the
first five years saw the planting of several thousand items
chosen for their density or fruit or form, so that birds and
small animals would have shelter from their natural predators, nesting sites near water, and food. Damaske planted
in large figure 8's wherever possible and in fence-line rows.
Henry and I, with Virginia and at least one of her friends,

chose small places here and there, and we used spuds, spades, and shovels, the choice of implement depending on the thickness of the turf.

About nine o'clock in the morning we gathered in the kitchen for instructions. Each person received his implement and some plants in a bucket. Virginia and her friends worked as a group, while Henry and I usually worked separately. For instance, once I set bittersweet vines at all the fence posts down the north side of the stream, while Henry planted clumps of red osier dogwood on the north banks of the stream. Virginia and Jeanne Larson and Billy Black set out black haws along the edge of the westernmost alfalfa field.

Some weekends were devoted to making brush piles so bunnies and woodchucks and quail would have winter protection. Since this brushing helped the appearance of the wood lots without destroying the dead wood, our labor served a double purpose.

"Place the largest pieces at the bottom," Henry instructed us, "so the pile won't collapse during the first winter. If you have a hollow log, be sure it's on the ground. Crisscross the smaller branches on that. Then cut some pine branches and lay them on top of the pile. Each pile will then be like an igloo."

We have had the satisfaction of seeing animals and birds run to these piles to escape owls, hawks, and foxes, and a woodchuck hibernated beneath the one nearest our porch. I watched him through my binoculars during the fall when he occasionally came out for food or a bit of sunshine. It was as if he could not make up his mind to begin his winter sleep as long as the silver maples above the brush were scattering their gold. Again in the early spring, when he was waking, I saw him emerge slowly from the dark underside of the brush, sit up and blink stupidly, then amble toward the feeder Henry had made beneath a near pine.

In late May the baby woodchucks are allowed to come out to play—indeed, they are pushed out by the mama. They tussle and romp almost like kittens, but at first they don't go more than about ten feet from the entrance to their den. Mama is usually sitting at the entrance to give warning if danger is approaching. In one second flat the whole family has disappeared down the hole.

One day, wanting to get a close picture of them, I crawled, flat on my stomach, to within some fifteen feet of the hole and readied my camera. After ten minutes a little head peeped out. Accepting me as part of the elderberry I was under, the baby came outside, followed by his siblings. I snapped three pictures before the mother appeared. Once outside, she realized something was amiss. She stood up and looked anxiously about. I snapped a shot of her in this posture, but she heard the click of the shutter and dived into the entrance. I heard no sound from her, but apparently the young ones did, for they scurried after.


One day I experienced wildlife from a supposedly tame animal. Virginia and Henry had gone on the tractor to a point where Henry wanted to roll some logs into the stream. I was sitting on the front steps with my binoculars, waiting for the appearance of two Swainson's hawks whose screeches had annoyed Henry.

Deer Run Farms had acquired a hundred head of beef cattle to fatten. Twice a steer had broken out of the pen, causing much annoyance to the farm hands and wasting valuable time. To buy a strong fast horse seemed to be a good idea. Philip Sawin and his manager, Stan Chilewski, selected a handsome white horse that had enough spirit and strength for three horses, but he proved to be of little value to them because no one but Howard Fravel could control him enough to mount, and Howard was in school except on weekends.

We had heard that Howard had had several narrow escapes from injury, for the horse was indeed wild. He trusted nobody. It was not until Howard's summer vacation that he could spend enough time with the animal to overcome a little of the horse's fear of man.

Howard had talked to me about trying to gain the animal's confidence.

"Somebody sure must have been hard on him. I talk to him all the time I'm putting hay in his bin and watering him. But I have to keep an eye on him all the time 'cause he's liable to turn quick and bite my shoulder. Twice I've had to jump over the fence to get away."

"Do you ever really ride him?" I asked.

"Oh, ya. I've rode him and I've sailed off him too. It's hard to tighten the girth if I do get a saddle on him. He has throwed me four times."

Then one day Howard reported that he had ridden Crazy Horse, as the farm hands had named him, on five successive days; the boy was confident that the animal was beginning to trust him.

"You have courage and patience," I said.

On this morning when I sat on the steps waiting to see the hawks, I was thinking that the recently pruned pines across the driveway might have been shorn too severely. Their few upper branches looked like shaggy wigs atop scrawny, knotty necks. But my musing was blasted by a sudden thunder of hoofs. My first thought was that Trig had got out of his pasture and was racing alone, as was his wont, but around the bend came the big white horse with Howard proudly astride a magnificent new saddle, tooled and bright with ornaments.

I stood up, admiring, and called a hello. Howard gently reined in the horse and walked him over to the red oak, intending to dismount and throw the reins over the yard pump, as Virginia did Trig's. But as he swung his right leg backward, the saddle girth gave a little and the horse jumped sideways, throwing Howard to the ground. His left foot caught momentarily in the stirrup and pulled the saddle still farther to the left.

The horse bolted toward the barn, stirrups and saddle sliding under his belly. One hind foot somehow got fastened in the cinch, and that horse went mad with fear!

I ran to help Howard, and the two of us stood breathless as the panic-stricken animal, on three legs, lunged straight for the solid side of the barn. Turning just in time to avoid a head-on crash, he disappeared behind the granary.

"He's ruinin' it, just ruinin' it!" Howard groaned. "Phil will kill me; he'll kill me. It's brand-new, just came an hour ago. Oh, mercy, I've got trouble a-plenty!"

We heard loud thuds, and the horse burst around the corner of the workshop, headed this time for us.

Now compared with a flea, I am not agile, but considered as a middle-aged woman, I'm not bad. In one leap I cleared the young cranberry bush and the peonies, caught the corner post, and swung myself up to the porch—just as that loco horse swooshed by and sprawled flat in my roses!

I get goose pimples even now as I write about it.

Howard had jumped behind the oak, but as soon as the brute fell, the boy ran to him and grabbed the bridle.

"You'll be killed!" I screamed.

He pinioned the animal's head close to his own body and talked very softly.

"Easy, boy, easy. Easy, boy, easy."

Though the horse was struggling to stand, Howard was loosening the cinch, carefully and swiftly. The saddle slowly slipped to the ground, freeing the entangled foot.

Without looking at the saddle, Howard moaned in a low voice to me, "Look at it. Is it hurt? Oh, mercy, why does everything happen to me? I do the best I know how."

I had never seen him so near tears.

"It's a little scratched, I think, and the stirrup strap is broken, but saddle oil will probably hide the scratches." My voice was shaky in spite of my effort to sound reassuring. "I'll bring the saddle to you in the car."

"I'll take it with me," he said forlornly. "I'll have to explain anyway."

The horse was standing, but the whites of his enormous eyes were still too conspicuous. Howard continued to talk softly to him and to stroke him. After a while he hoisted the heavy, dusty saddle to his shoulder. I winced, but he didn't. Picking up the reins, he walked toward the driveway. Crazy Horse, rolling his eyes and trembling, followed his only friend.

I sank to the steps then and wept a little with relief that Howard had not been seriously hurt. Admiration for him, for his understanding of and pity for the fear-ridden brute, swelled my breast, and sympathy for the boy in his bad luck tightened my throat. That crazy horse! But then a new idea came to me. If he had been completely without reason in his flight, he would have continued to run away from Howard, but he hadn't. He had come back. Like a tornado, it was true, but he had come back. He would not have returned to the boy if he had not begun to trust him. Somehow

his confused and warped brain had absorbed the truth that
this man was kind. In his horrible new dilemma, with the
hated heavy object swinging under his belly and holding
one of his feet, he must have thought Howard could help
him. So he had plunged and leapt his way back to him.
While Howard was holding the horse's head down, he had
taken hold of Howard's arm with his teeth, but he hadn't
bitten.

Maybe there's hope yet, I thought.

The next weekend I drove over to Deer Run Farms and
asked Stan about both the boy and the horse.

"Oh, Howard has moved over to Pleasant Lake. He's got
a summer job at the bowling alley. And Crazy Horse? That
doggone horse isn't here any more. Phil sold him, thank
God!"


After that experience the woodsy wildlife seemed tame to
me—until one night when I had elected to remain on the
farm with only Happy for company and protection. Henry
and Virginia had to return to Madison that Sunday night,
but Henry wanted to come back to the farm early the next
morning. I decided I was brave enough to stay alone, though
that summer no one lived in the Warren house. By road the
nearest neighbor was a mile away. But I was not easily
frightened, and I was physically weary after a long hike, so
that I wanted to go to sleep early.

"I'll be all right," I assured Henry. "Your rifle and shotgun
are here, and Happy will let me know if a stranger appears.
Don't worry about me. I'd rather stay alone than make that
seventy-five miles tonight and again tomorrow morning."

I fed Happy while the sky was still mauve and rose from
the sunset, and then I took him out to his pen. When I

returned to the kitchen, I watched Ed Sullivan's program on the new television set that Henry had insisted on buying "to keep you company while I fish for mayflies." Mayfly fishing is best in the early hours of darkness during June; he was often gone until about eleven o'clock. However, the set had been in the house for a month, and this was the first night I had watched a program.

I locked the four exterior doors, drew water for my bath, and walked into the living room to select a magazine to read in bed for a little while. Suddenly I froze with fear as a terrified scream came from the general region of Happy's pen.

I turned off the light and hurried to the front door. After listening there for a minute, I unlocked and opened it enough to press my face against the screen. Again that awful shriek rent the air. It couldn't be an animal, I thought. Yet could it be human? Happy had not barked; he surely would have, had strangers come around. The wild shriek came again, closer, this time nearer the pen. I had goose pimples all over my arms and I couldn't bat my eyes. Then it came again, and I knew it was in a tree! My fear vanished as suddenly as it had come. I unlocked the screen door and walked quietly to the end of the porch. It had to be a bird, but what kind? It was in agony; of that I was certain. A fifth time the screech came, this time down by the stream. Yes, it had to be a bird.

I went back indoors, filled with wonder. It had to be a powerful bird, perhaps the biggest owl, the great horned. But what could have happened to it? Finding the Audubon book, I read about that bird; one sentence was, "Its scream, a loud terrifying sound, is seldom heard." But no explanation was given for its utterance.

Later that year our Beloit friend, Ira Kurth, told me that

he had once heard the same kind of cry from a great horned owl when a weasel had it by the throat. A weasel doesn't let go of its victim. An owl, whose weapon is its beak, is helpless to fight if its attacker has a hold just beneath the beak. I accepted Ira's verdict.

Henry and I saw a weasel one morning as we ate breakfast. Brown like mink, he fooled us for a while. But his darting movements and his wild expression made us decide he was a weasel, reported to be the most vicious predator in these parts. He sped across the rocks, disappeared under a plantain lily, popped up in the pinks, scooted over a mat of ajuga, scurried among the leaves, and slithered down a gopher's hole, but was up again in a flash. He stood up to scan the scene; then he ran through the *Iris cristata* so fast he resembled a snake.

"I hope the chipmunk doesn't come out of *his* hole just now," I whispered to Henry.

*Sedum spectabile* hid Chippy's entrance, else the marauder surely would have seen it.

"He'd be safer outside than in his hole if the weasel goes into it," Henry observed.

"Yes, he could run up a tree, but weasels climb too."

"They raid birds' nests and eat young squirrels. No young thing is safe from them. Darrell told me one got into their duck yard and killed seven full-grown ducks, and Leo Schroeder said he loses several hens to weasels each year. They're absolutely fearless."

Ira later told us he had seen a weasel attack a water snake three times his size. "And he'll eat every bit of his victim," said Ira. "He sucks blood and eats bones as well as flesh and skin. He's not above earthy small things either, like worms and mice and even ants and mosquitoes. Oh, there's no doubt about a weasel's being the worst predator of all."

"I suppose hawks and owls are his natural enemies?" I asked.

"And fox," said Henry.

Ira said he had once found a cat carrying a dead weasel! We were astonished at that.

"She probably had sat all night at his burrow waiting for him to come home from his nightly search. Maybe he was so full and content that he was careless as he approached. The cat dropped him when she saw me. His neck had been broken; the cat had apparently used the weasel's own method for killing."

I looked in Seton's *Wild Animals I Have Known* to see what kind of weasel we had. It was the long-tailed New York weasel. It turns white in winter, when it is called ermine; I hope to see one some day in that color stage.

Henry asked the Fenskes what to plant to tide the game birds and deer and squirrels over the winter. We had noticed a scarcity of acorns the preceding season, and we had heard that squirrels by the dozens had swum the Mississippi River to spend the winter in Iowa, where the acorn crop was more plentiful.

"Buckwheat and corn," said Darrell.

"Yes, buckwheat and corn will stand up above the snow," said his father. "They've high yield and contain the basic nourishment needs for most of the game animals."

We were standing by the bridge and looking at the field nearest their fence.

"Tell you what," said Harold, "I'll put some corn in here for you when I plant mine, and we'll let it stand. Darrell traps on your land, and all three of us fish your stream and hunt your land, so I'll put in a quarter-acre of corn for you.

I'd put it on mine, but I need the crop. Long's you got the land and not planting it——"

"By all means," said Henry, "I'd like that. Plant as much as you will. Corn will be good for deer and pheasant."

"If the squirrels leave them any," said Darrell.

"A quarter-acre will help a lot of game survive a rough spell," said Henry, "but I've got more land than that, so you plant as much as you want to."

It was April, and the past winter had been a hard one. We had come up once in January and twice in February to put out seed and suet in the two feeding stations Henry had built according to a plan he had found in the *Conservation Bulletin.* This Easter vacation time gave us the opportunity to look for the wildlife that had survived. The deer we saw were on the thin side but not really haggard like those farther north, according to reports we heard at Wichner's Store. Only one gray squirrel came around during our ten days, and Henry scared up only two grouse. We heard no pheasant calls and saw no woodcock.

Henry built more feeding stations. This time he made them like the ready-made ones he could have bought at a good hardware store: similar to an inverted bucket in a pie-plate topped by a canopy. The first ones had been built with heavy cardboard over wooden platforms. Snow and ice did not damage the cardboard, but rain during April and May did. So he substituted sheets of tin, tying them to the pine branches overhead.

"Quail are my chief concern," said Henry. "If they are not able to dig through the snow for seed, they'll freeze to death. Big birds can find corn buried in a foot of snow, but quail can't. And if they don't eat for two weeks they die."

He placed several feeders near the house so we could

watch the birds and animals using them; the others he placed on Jack Pine Hill near the drive, where he could fill them easily even when the snow lay deep. Currants, black cherries, Solomon's-seal berries, rose hips, and wild plum grow in that area; so do hazelnuts, alders, and birch, which provide catkins for the grouse. Indeed, this is the ruffed grouse's best-loved area unless it be the fen east of Birch Pond, which offers the same menu and is more secluded.

"Deer, too, will eat here when they're hungry," said Henry. "What we do for one species of wildlife seems to help all the others."

I thought of the fate of several bird boxes made for us by Ira. He intended them as homes for bluebirds, wrens, and swallows. We selected proper sites: fence posts and stumps at the edge of woodland and orchard for the bluebird houses, workshop and granary walls for the wren boxes, and tree trunks nearer the alfalfa fields for the swallows. But alas, squirrels, both gray and red, took over a third of them. They gnawed the entrances large enough to accommodate themselves and nested in the small interiors. The reds were the more numerous home thieves; before, they had been accustomed to build in treetops far away from the farmhouse, stripping cedars of their bark for ten feet from the ground to use in building their summer homes in crotches forty to fifty feet up.

The habits of gray squirrels are much the same, both squirrels preferring a sheltered barn loft or abandoned chicken house to the tree site. Two grays raised their young in the straw above the rabbit hutch. In years gone by, four feet of packed straw in the low attic had served as insulation for rabbits. The smart little squirrels discovered this comfortable place and gnawed an opening in the eaves; from that they tunneled a pathway and hollowed out a "bedroom."

One day I was surprised to see three small faces lined up at an opening inside the hutch. They were obviously squirrel babies. I had to laugh, they were so cunning and pretty. A fourth and larger face then appeared, and all four vanished into darkness. I tiptoed to the spot and listened. Only a scratchy sound and a faint peep, more like that of a bird, did I hear.

We are using the hutch as a catchall for the small pieces of horse-drawn machinery and obsolete farm tools, one of the early wooden-and-tin washing machines, a few old broken chairs, and such. I call it the Broken-Parted Museum. Some day I may make it into a studio. The walls are stuccoed, the floor is concrete; it is a well-lighted room with four windows and is wired for electricity. The trouble is the ceiling, which is too uneven to cover with either Sheetrock or planks or insulating tile. The rough beams are exposed, and each is a different thickness from the others. At present straw falls through the cracks. We could easily block the holes or poison the squirrels, but if we did, would they not then take over the bluebird houses attached to the outside walls?

For the past two years we have had flying squirrels also, and these cunning rodents have made their homes exclusively in the bluebird boxes. However, because these squirrels are rare and because they are easily tamed, we hope they stay with us and multiply. To this end I often place bread, ground meat, nuts, and apple cores on the tops of their boxes. When Ted Weis was a senior at the University, Virginia gave him a young flying squirrel. He often took it with him, asleep in his breast pocket; in zoology class he would tickle it surreptitiously, and it would awaken and poke its head out the top of the pocket, to the startled amusement of those who happened to glance his way.

At the farm we can hear them landing on the roof in the evenings, scurrying about on the tin as they play. We sit out sometimes in the lawn chairs beneath the big red oak to watch them. Brownish gray on top, they are pure white beneath, and can be seen easily as they swing about in the air, making fantastic leaps, some so long that I can scarcely refrain from squealing for fear the little daredevils will fall. I forget that their "wings," the folds of skin and fur running along their sides, prevent falls.

Our deer are the Virginia white-tails. It is a thrill to hear a snort and a thump and to see a flash of bright white as a startled animal takes off at challenging speed. Usually he crawls under fences, but when frightened, he leaps over. Once when Virginia and I surprised a buck about to cross Warren Road at the Wedde, he took the road in one leap and both the five-foot bank and three-foot fence in a second leap!

Again, during a deer season, when all deer are nervous and weary from running for their lives, another buck at the same place fell on the icy road as he attempted the same feat; I stopped my car to wait until he had scrambled up the bank and slipped under the fence. I hoped he'd find rest in the nook I had found one day on a walk; just over the rise a boulder left by the glacier juts out from the hillside, and soil has been washed away from beneath it, leaving a small cave hidden by silky dogwood. Surely the buck knew of the hideout, and I hoped he'd take refuge there until rested. As I drove on, though, a shot rang out. A hunter had found it first.

Later Howard came over, greeting us with a victorious smile. "I got mine. Did Henry get his?"

"Not yet," I said. "Where did you get yours?"

"In our woods. Do you know where the big boulder is?"

I nodded. "I think I heard your shot."

"Now my brother's family will have venison all winter. Trudi has never tasted it."

Trudi was a German girl who married Chuck Fravel while he was stationed in her country following World War II. She had won the hearts of Chuck's family by her gentle ways, her humor, and her good cooking. It was understandable that Howard was happy to bring home a supply of meat for her and the family.

"He'll dress out at about a hundred and fifty pounds," Howard went on.

"If Henry gets one, I hope it's no heavier," I said. "They're so much more tender and flavorful if they are from a hundred to a hundred and fifty. Do you grind up a good deal of the meat, Howard, or do you cut it up in the conventional pattern?"

"Oh, we grind a lot and mix it with ground pork for breakfast patties."

"Henry has got his deer each season for about seven years," I boasted. "He butchers it in Madison in our basement. I wrap and label each piece and place it in our freezer. We like the chops and steaks best, so he cuts all he can into those. We give the neck to friends who like to make mincemeat of it, and we grind the rest. This year maybe we'll have a market grind a good deal more and mix it with pork. Since all you Richford folks seem to like it best that way, it must be good."

Howard rubbed his stomach. "I'm already hungry for it.

By the way, where's Virginia? She didn't go hunting with Henry, did she?"

"No. She's spending the day with Arla. She's trying to persuade Arla to remain in school. The girl's in love and wants to drop out to get married."

"I know. She's just sixteen too. The law says you don't have to go after you're sixteen. Most every boy around here drops out then, but I'm still going and hope to finish next June."

Arla did drop out of high school, and she married her sweetheart, who lived in Wautoma. That was the end of the companionship between the two girls. It had been an enriching relationship for nine years; indeed, I like to think it enriched their whole lives.

Deer were numerous that November in Waushara County. At Wichner's Store we heard farmers complaining of damage done to their corn before it could be harvested.

"I had a half-acre of berries last year," said Arthur Schaube, "and durn if them deer didn't dig down and eat 'em under the snow!"

"All six in my family's hunting every day the whole nine days," declared George Schlay. "We aim to get as many's we can. We got a party permit too."

The party permit is issued to a group of four who want to hunt together; each hunter is allowed to kill one buck for himself, and a fifth deer, of either sex, is allowed for the party. In actual practice it sometimes happens that the best hunter shoots several deer, not just his own. After getting his own, he stays with the party to help the others get theirs. He can shoot all five if he's that lucky, but he cannot keep them for his own family.

To injure a deer and not be able to kill him is a constant anxiety to Henry during the season, for he has at times found an animal that has died a slow death after a fatal injury. For that reason he will not shoot unless he has a clear view and is close enough to feel sure his shot will be true. He sights his rifle in at two hundred and fifty yards but tries to be closer than that. Once he wounded a buck and could not find him in the dense brush along our creek. He drove seven miles to find Darrell and ask him and the other Fenskes to help find the injured animal. After a half-hour search, they found him; he had died in the edge of the water after running just a few yards. Henry's shot had entered his neck.

Bow-and-arrow season opens in September and lasts into December, with a reprieve during the rifle season in late November. Henry goes out with his bow, but he won't let an arrow fly if the animal is more than thirty yards away unless the deer is standing instead of running. As a result, he rarely gets a chance. The weather and the countryside are so beautiful during bow season that, as Henry puts it, "just being out is recompense enough, deer or no deer." He has the woods pretty much to himself, since few farmers hunt with bow. During rifle season, on the other hand, one has to watch out for careless hunters even more than for deer.

Rifle season is always an exciting and colorful time. I look forward to it, though I never hunt. We get up before dawn, at four-thirty, in fact. It is important that Henry reach his "stand" before the appointed time, which is thirty minutes before sunrise. While he dresses in his bright vermilion woolen suit and pulls on his hunting boots over two pairs of wool socks and his insulated underwear, I stir up the latent coals in the iron range and add kindling, working by candlelight in order not to warn deer that might be feeding near the house.

I prepare the poached eggs, sausage, and coffee.

"Come and get it!" I sing out, but not very loudly.

We eat in the dim light, and when he is ready to go I hand him a small thermos of coffee to warm him after an hour in the cold.

One time, when Virginia was fourteen, she went with him, dressed in red from crown to heel. But when they left the house, the red could have been black in the predawn darkness. I was uneasy for fear they'd shoot each other before the light of dawn could show up the color—no, not really afraid of that, for I knew Henry would not shoot unless he could see antlers, and he had taught Virginia how important it was not to shoot at just movement.

"Sit or stand still until sunup," I said to them.

Virginia folded her hands and rolled her eyes. "May Artemis of the Chase protect us!" This was her first hunt, and she was going just to please her father.

They went that morning to Emil Wiesjahn's swamp. Henry directed Virginia to sit beside a big stump along the deer trail. He went around to Randall's woods and took a stand at the other end of the same trail. She told me later that she thought her seat and her feet had frozen before she dared move; it was 15° Fahrenheit.

At dawn she saw what looked like antlers on a deer up the trail. Her heart beating fast and hard, she aimed her gun and flicked off the safety. For a full minute she held the aim; then she lowered the gun a trifle, remembering that even if the deer came closer, she couldn't lawfully shoot before five-thirty.

"I strained my eyes at my watch," she told me when she came home, "but my vision blurred. I thought my eyeballs had frozen from staring so hard at him. When I looked up again, the antlers were only part of a rotten limb and the deer only a stump!"

That was her solitary attempt at deer hunting. Perhaps Pete was the chief reason she wouldn't go again.

Pete was a wild fawn that came up to Howard Fravel one day when he was in his barn. Howard fed it milk from his niece's baby bottle. It came back the next day, and Howard was feeding it as Virginia rode up on Trig. He let her hold the bottle. The fawn was clumsy but managed to get every drop of milk. Then he licked her fingers and sucked her elbow. Howard bedded him down with the cows in warm straw.

"The mother must be dead," Howard said, "or injured. Pete is as hungry today as he was yesterday." Howard walked through his woods looking for the doe in likely places—clumps of tall meadow grass, pine and cedar groves, and hollows. Virginia rode through similar places. But they found no clue.

Henry laughed at them. "Pete's just playing you for a good thing. His mother's not dead. He's just getting two meals instead of one."

Howard mixed a formula Virginia had found in one of her zoology books: equal parts water and whole milk plus one-half teaspoon each of brewer's yeast and edible bone meal. Pete was fed that daily until he was ready for solid food, then they gave him mash and whole-wheat bread. Soon he was browsing for himself, preferring our new planting of white cedar.

He slept some in Fravels' barn during the day, but he seemed to roam all night; perhaps he returned to his mother at twilight and the two of them roamed together. At any rate, he grew fast and endeared himself to both our families. He sometimes followed Virginia and Trig down the road, and one night when Henry was mowing alfalfa by the light of his tractor, Pete appeared at the edge of the field to stare.

When school began in September, Pete boarded the school bus one morning, to the immense delight of the children and the consternation of the driver. When the hunting season came, though, Howard and Virginia were anxious about their pet.

"I could shut him up in the barn," said Howard.

"That's against the law," Virginia reminded him.

"It's a spike-buck season too."

They looked at the little rounded spikes showing about an inch above Pete's skull. His legs were so long that he seemed older than he was. But there was nothing to be done to safeguard him; so Pete took his chances with his cousins, and none of us ever saw him again.

Virginia would not talk about him, but she said she'd never again hunt deer.

In recent deer seasons Henry has hunted our farm almost exclusively. Our pines have grown well and now afford much protection for the animals and birds. A deer can run through them for a long way without being seen by a hunter. Henry, however, knows of an opening across which deer run when frightened by hunters in the state-owned Lackelt farm acreage. For two years the same hunter there has shot at a deer in our east field, and the animal has run into the opening near Henry, who has brought him down with a true shot.

After the second incident the man came up to Henry and

said, "Well, if I do that every year, I suppose you won't mind my trespassing on your property!"

"Nope," said Henry while fastening his tag on the knee tendon of one of the deer's hind legs. "Do it again next year in precisely this way. But I'd appreciate your letting me know which day you're to be here."

The man nodded with a wry smile and left without identifying himself. The next year we think he remained on the state-owned land; Darrell came across a man jubilantly dressing a deer, and the description fitted our unknown visitor.

Sometimes farmer neighbors in groups of four or five will come to the house and ask permission to drive through our land. We always say yes. Henry is usually asked to be one of the standers, for he is known as a good shot. The one man of the group who is to be a stander remains with Henry, and they tell the others exactly where they will be waiting. The drivers then get into their car and go around by the road to the east. They park the car and enter our land from that area, driving through our pines toward the spot where Henry and the other man are standing. Virginia and I stay inside the house and away from the windows. We can hear an occasional halloo and a shouting from the drivers to frighten deer out of hiding. Soon the red coats materialize out of the greenery, and if they are not too eager to "shove on," I serve coffee. They are too warmly dressed, though, to remain indoors for more than four or five minutes.

"It's so exciting!" exclaimed Virginia one day as we watched them hurry away.

"I wonder whether the danger they're in or the color of their clothes is the reason for our excitement," I said.

"It's their own spirit," said Virginia. "They have forgot

all their troubles and those of the world. Nothing matters except adventure and comradeship. They all seem so happy! Did you notice how Dad glows in their presence? He must get awfully tired of us women."

"Oh, I think he likes us all right. He doesn't want to come up here alone, you know."

About an hour later I looked out at the frozen pool. A young buck was walking along the north bank! I called to Virginia, and we watched him as he turned into the alders not far from one of Henry's lowland stands. We listened for a shot, and pretty soon we heard it. Just one. Then we opened the back door and called to Henry.

"Did you get him?"

We heard an answer, but we couldn't tell whether it was a "Ya!" or a "Naw!" With our binoculars we saw a commotion upstream near Fenskes' line. So we called again. Then we saw Henry running toward the house. When he was within a hundred yards, he shouted, "I got him. I'm going to get the tractor to pull him home with."

After he had dragged the dead deer to the parking area, we donned our warm red parkas and ran out to congratulate him and to judge the age of the deer, for if it were the young one we had seen, we could be sure of tender meat.

With a block and tackle Henry hoisted the dressed-out carcass to a beam in the implement shed, where it hung for two days while Henry hunted with Harold Fenske. When the flesh began to freeze, Henry said he'd rather butcher it before it was frozen too hard. So we tied the carcass to the top of the car and went home to Madison.

Though I see many fox holes in the wooded hillsides and the sandy fields, I seldom see a fox. Red fox travel high ground, avoiding the low spots and brush, but they have

beaten the prairie grasses into well-defined paths to all-year
open water. Henry sees them while he is fishing. Last year
he shot at one on the pond bank, and we saw a young one
bounding after a rabbit, which found sanctuary beneath—
where else?—the rabbit hutch. The fox was a handsome
animal, a rich brown-red with an extraordinarily full brush,
which he carried high while running the rabbit. The white
tip of the tail looked like a plume.

"Oh, he's too pretty to kill!" I exclaimed.

Henry watched him, too, and made no movement for his
gun.

"Darrell will probably get him next winter in one of his
traps," he said, and his prediction was right. Darrell caught
twenty-six in traps he set on the Fenske land and ours. The
bounty was three dollars that year.

We seem to have no gray fox at Triple Ridge, though
Henry has seen them on other farms. He sees both red and
gray during deer season, when he is outdoors continuously
for hours. He doesn't shoot them at that time, however, for
he'd give away his position. Indeed, he is not a serious hunter
of fox at any time, for he feels as I do, that fox and other
predators will be controlled by natural factors. However, we
do understand the concern of our neighbors who lose their
chickens, young pigs, lambs, geese, and ducks to fox, the
number of which has increased in spite of the bounty.

"They ought to have a bigger bounty," said Darrell, "so
everybody'd hunt 'em. They'd go out for fox, not just get
one incidental-like while hunting for something else. Three
dollars is too low. Five dollars would be better."

"Sportsmen, too, should be concerned," added his brother.
"All these Conservation Department pheasants that are released so hunters will have something to shoot at—the hunters get very few of them; yet next year there aren't any, or

not many anyway. Know why? Fox. They don't always eat them either, right then; they bury them in brush for rougher times later in the winter."

"Wouldn't there be fewer fox," Henry wanted to know, "if the habitat for their victims were improved? If mice and birds could find shelter close at hand, they'd escape their predators. Then the predators would die off."

"Might be something in that," agreed Howard.

"But," said Darrell, "if there weren't enough wildlife for the fox, they'd eat even more of our farm stock!"

"Might be something in that," said Henry.

Then they laughed and turned to the hot blueberry muffins and cold milk I had brought out.

I suppose every wild-meat eater is considered a predator, and it is customary for man, particularly here in the United States, to think of him with dislike and even repulsion sometimes; but some authorities say that meat-eaters do less harm to the world than do vegetal-feeders.

Mid-October is the best time in central Wisconsin to get color-happy. That's when the maples are most riotous and profligate and the birches and basswoods vie in putting out the most pure gold. One October fifteenth I took Dorothy Ratcliff to the farm with me to see our red and yellow valley. Walking through the lowlands, we saw a striped grass snake; I was surprised, for I thought snakes had gone into hibernation a few weeks earlier.

At the farmhouse Virginia greeted us with another snake in a bottle. Henry had brought it to show to her. Turning the bottle upside down, she let the very small snake, six inches long and as thick as a string of spaghetti, slide out into her hand.

"It's a red-bellied snake, a mature one. This is as long as it will ever grow," she declared.

Dorothy stepped behind me as she gave a strange little moan.

"Oh, he's harmless," Virginia assured her. The snake curled around her finger and was quiet. "Do you want to hold him, Mother?"

"No, thank you." I could not forget a similar-looking snake, the deadly coral, that inhabits the eastern part of Texas; indeed, it is all over the Southland, I think.

We have no poisonous snakes, for which we're thankful. Several kinds of grass snakes live in our meadows, and the brown and red water snake lives along the stream, but, though we are outdoors so very much, we seldom see one. The water snake is a mean-looking creature, and his bite is rather painful, they say, but it isn't fatal. Once, while Henry was resting from fishing, he leaned against a high bank while he ate his sandwich; soon he became conscious of a movement at the small of his back. When he turned, he saw he had backed up against a fat water snake. He killed it, but not because he was afraid of it; he didn't want it to eat his young trout.

Virginia once found a snake that had choked to death on a trout too large for him. Our late friend, Chubby Goodlad, once brought us a trout that had choked to death on a young snake too large for him!

So it goes.

Skunks have given us some trouble. We've had to practice management on them, but we don't mind having them on the farm. Skunks, like raccoons, weasels, and flying squirrels, are chiefly nocturnal. We don't often see them unless we get up at dawn and stand watch near their holes. We're not that eager to make their acquaintance, but circumstances sometimes take over.

The kitchen ell of the farmhouse has crawl space beneath it; only the two-story part of the house has a full basement. The crawl space is bricked in, and the two ventilators are screened against just what occurred. Skunks built their winter home underneath the kitchen. This happened the first winter after we moved into the house. For a while we thought the butane gas was leaking; the Coloma agent obligingly came out and carefully checked the cookstove, the Servel refrigerator, and the water heater. When he put a daub of his soap mixture on each gas jet, not a bubble appeared to indicate a leak. Some hours after he left, the smell annoyed us again. For three weekends we noticed it and were bewildered. I began to wonder whether it was inherent in the old house itself. Maybe we'd never be rid of it.

Howard Fravel came over early one Saturday before I had aired the kitchen.

"What are you going to do about your skunks?" he asked.

Henry and I stared at each other.

"What *can* we do?" Henry asked.

"Nothing much. Ignore 'em or kill 'em."

"With traps?"

"Better a gun, a shotgun—so you'll be sure the first time."

He lay down on the sand beside the porch steps and edged his slender body under.

"Here's their hole," he called. "They've dug under the bricks."

Crouching, we peered into the semi-darkness and could barely see the pile of sand around their entrance.

"That ties it," said Henry.

Next morning he got up before dawn and took his stand

in the door of his workshop to await the return of Mr. or Mrs. Skunk. We hoped one of them had been out foraging. The workshop is southeast of the house and across the driveway, far enough away to fool an animal near the house porch into thinking no danger would come to him from that building about a hundred feet away.

I sat beside the kitchen window in the dark house. When I looked toward the workshop I could see Henry's lighted cigarette.

After the first gray light came, Henry's keen eyes saw a skunk moving slowly but purposefully around the southeast corner of the house. When it was silhouetted against the light-gray cellar doors, he shot once. I jumped up and stood just inside the door until I heard him call, "I got him!" Even then I didn't open the door, for I expected an onslaught of the skunk's offensive munition. None came, however, for death had been instantaneous.

Henry brought a carton and lifted the handsome black and white animal into it.

"He's beautiful," I said, "and so gentle looking. I don't wonder that Ernest Thompson Seton declared he liked skunks and always had one or more for pets. But I bet he didn't have them under his cabin floor. Maybe he had sinus trouble and couldn't smell them. At one time," I went on while Henry placed the carton in the trailer with other cartons of trash to take to the Dump, "at one time Seton suggested that the U.S.A. accept the skunk instead of the eagle as its emblem because the skunk is peculiar to this continent and is a good citizen, minding its own business, harming no one, habitually inoffensive—unless greatly angered or frightened. But Seton failed to secure sufficient support."

"Good," said Henry.

The next weekend I stayed alone at the farm one night and let Happy sleep indoors. At dawn I got up and let him out, but he stopped on the porch and stiffened. Walking toward the steps was another big skunk! I stood transfixed just inside the open screen door. When Happy began to bark, I got hold of my voice and frantically urged him back into the kitchen. But he was going to protect his mistress against this strange big cat, come what may—poor dog.

The skunk continued ambling toward us with her eyes on him.

"Happy! Come here! Happy!" I reached out to get him by his short curly tail, but he lunged at the skunk; she swung her body and lifted her tail, and I slid in front of the boots cabinet to be out of the line of fire.

She let him have her musk full in the face. He fell backwards, then bounded high over her and rolled in the grass, scraping his face in agony. Then he ran for the pool, jumped in, and swam about, ducking his head over and over. That was the best thing he could have done for himself, for it washed the musk from his eyes. After a while I took a handful of ground meat to him, but with a stick I gently fended him off me. I spoke reassuringly to him but didn't let him follow me back to the house, and I decided to forgo the pleasure of my daily hour in the hammock since he would want to lie near me. I saw him swimming frequently the rest of the morning.

When Henry came at noon and I told him of the incident, he took a large can of tomato juice from my shelves and went down to the pool to bathe the dog in it. There seems to be nothing better for dispelling the odor of skunk. Then Henry lay in the hammock, with Happy chained to a young oak a few feet away. After a half hour Henry took the dog to the edge of the water and washed off the juice; then he let him run free of the leash as they both returned to the house.

In the meantime I had scrubbed the steps and porch with suds and an old broom and rinsed them with the water hose. Happy, though, refused to enter, and I was pleased that he had such sensitivity, for I wasn't so sure as his master was that his odor was gone.

Though Henry, after shooting the first skunk, had filled the hole beneath the porch with sand, this one had obviously redug it. We couldn't know whether she had worked from the outside or the inside; her tracks were quite apparent from the steps to the hole.

"I'll borrow a trap," Henry said. He hated to use one because of the suffering it causes an animal if not tended often. "We'll be here for two more mornings, and we can take it up before we leave if we catch nothing."

Virginia and Fritz drove up in the "hearse" about mid-afternoon, and I described the day's events to them.

"I can't smell anything," said Virginia, sniffing, "but then, I have a slight cold."

Fritz sniffed too. "It doesn't smell like violets yet," he said.

When all of us were ready to go to bed, Henry set the trap near the steps. The next morning we slept until eight o'clock; then Henry anxiously inspected the trap.

"It hasn't been sprung," he reported. "I'll leave it there all morning if you and Virginia will be careful. I'm taking Fritz with me to work on a revetment downstream."

About midmorning I walked from the rear terrace to the front yard, intending to water the *Vinca minor* in front of the peonies. About ten feet from the steps a skunk was dragging the trap! I ran back to the terrace, went into the living room, where Virginia was studying, and told her to get her father's shotgun.

"It's not in the gun rack," she said. "I'll use the twenty-two."

"Oh no! You might miss him with that." She was as fine a shot as her father, but a small target is, after all, harder to hit with a rifle than with a shotgun.

She was already out the rear door, and I followed. She hurried to the front yard and, approaching the skunk carefully, shot him in the head.

As with the other skunk, the relaxing glands emitted only a faint, really not unpleasant odor. It was a bit like that of crushed leaves of bog-grown plants. (That is why the handsome swamp cabbage is called skunk cabbage.)

Several times that day we knelt on the ground at the ventilators and listened for sounds of other animals. We feared there might be babies, for it was May, when ordinarily the young are born. We became convinced there were none, but I wondered what we would have done had there been some. Having heard a skunk is easy to train and can be deodorized, Virginia had long wanted one for a pet. Henry and I would have been loath to kill the babies but more reluctant to add them to the menagerie already at home in Madison: turtles, tropical fish, white mice, a parakeet, and a Siamese cat—not to mention Happy, who demanded more attention than all the others together.

Soon we had another family of skunks under one of the poultry houses; they dug out a cave so big that the thin concrete floor caved in. However, since we don't need that building, we let them have it. Howard Fravel told us skunks are valuable to farmers in keeping down the destructive mouse population, and we know they eat grubs and beetles, potato bugs particularly, and grasshoppers.

"But, Howard," I said, "they also eat cultivated fruit and they rob birds' nests!"

"Ya, but potatoes and corn are more important than fruit and birds," he answered.

Badgers are here, according to local storytellers, but we haven't seen any. And bear stories are sometimes told at Wichner's Store. Some late drinkers claimed they saw a bear in the Richford cemetery as they left the tavern one Saturday night. A Dakota farmer, seven miles east of Richford, claimed he found a bear track in his apiary. But we doubt that bear exist this far south of the Canadian border.

Raccoons we have in quantity. Henry sees them while he is fishing, and Darrell has trapped them along the stream. The little ones, with their funny black masks, look as if they're playing a game and are all made up with black mascara. Henry says they are an amusing sight when playing hide-and-seek, or when they play peek-a-boo with him around a stump. (Our fur-farm pen was originally constructed for one of the Wentland boys to use for raising raccoons.)

Marjorie and Henry Hill, also of the University faculty, sometimes walk to our farm by way of the stream. They own twenty-five acres and an attractive cottage about two miles to the east of us. Once, as they approached our land, they saw a family of coons coming from a den oak. Henry and I went in search of them after the Hills had gone. Walking about fifty feet apart, we stepped quietly and slowly along, looking at all the dead limbs and holes in the tree trunks, and we finally found the right tree, an oak with one live branch at the top. Eight feet from the ground was the opening, with the bark missing from a circle about four inches wider than the opening. From there to the ground were splotches of bare trunk scraped smooth by the scrambling of many feet. A faint trail could be distinguished from den to stream. With ear to trunk we listened, but there was no giveaway sound.

In a storm during the early summer that tree fell. The coons are still in the area, but we have not yet found their new home.

Darrell came up to the house one day with an otter he had killed on our stream. Earlier he had trapped its mate. We had not seen an otter before, nor found one of their typical "slides," which they make when sliding down to the water to escape an enemy or just for fun.

"He's awfully big," I observed while this one was lying at my feet. "He must be four feet long if you count his flattened tail."

"The other one was big, too," said Darrell proudly. "They've done away with a lot of trout, I guess."

Virginia stood silent and sad.

"Yes," said Henry, "otter's chief food is fish. I'm glad you got them."

When the men had taken the animal away, Virginia said to me, "Otters are simply enchanting animals. They play games all their lives; they skate on ice, and they wrestle with each other, and they take turns on their 'slides.' Oh, why do men want to *kill* everything?"

"In this case it's the bounty, I think. Otter fur brings a good price, second only to that of mink."

The woodchucks that lived in the brush pile near our porch were a continuing source of study, or rather observation, for me. An afternoon in October one remained outside his burrow for an hour and a half, ambling around among the pines—certainly no verdurous area for him—and then he waddled to the cherry bush vicinity, nibbled at clover, and uprooted some anemones and feasted on their tender roots. Through my binoculars I could see how frightened he always looked when he sat up to scout for danger. Also, when he looked straight ahead he seemed frightened. Only when he was nibbling did he relax.

Somehow I felt this was not the mother woodchuck I had watched in June. Though this one weighed about eight pounds, I felt he was probably one of the litter born six months before and that he was probably going to remain near his birthplace for the winter. His siblings and parents had moved, apparently. Perhaps he was the timid brother who needed to stay in familiar surroundings. He'd hibernate here, sleeping the sleep of the near-dead. On groundhog day, the second of February, I was pretty sure he'd still be unconscious and would not appear above ground to see his shadow, for this is Wisconsin, where spring never comes in February.

Virginia brought moles, shrews, and salamanders to show me, and then she let them go. The salamander that she found in the leaf-filled pit around the yard pump was, we thought, a wise one; in the declivity he had a perfect home, with the moisture and darkness that he loved and unquestioned safety from predators. (We had put leaves into the pit to act as insulation for the pipe and pump cylinder.)

We marveled at the very large forefeet of the mole, at the lack of eyes and ears on this tiny, incredibly soft, gray creature only six inches long. His powerful forepaws, three-quarters of an inch wide, dig extensive tunnels every night.

"How long are they?" I wanted to know.

"Let's measure the one he was caught in," Virginia suggested.

By noting the moisture retained in the sand, we could tell

which was freshly dug and which had been dug the night before. The latest tunnel ran in a devious route from the area of the pump to the rock wall below the terrace; it was seventy-six feet long!

"Well," I sighed after our two hours of digging and re-placing grass, "I hope his catch of cutworms, wireworms, and such made up for the appearance of my lawn."

"He has to eat more than his weight," said Virginia. "He digs near the roots of plants for worms. That's why he should never be killed. He's really valuable to have around."

"Most people think he eats the roots too," I said.

"No, he doesn't, my books say. But gardeners can see that he has been working in their beds. So, when their plants die, they think he has caused them to. It's the worms that have killed them, the worms he didn't find."

The shrews are very dark brown and not even as long as the mole. Virginia gently laid back the fur of one to show me the minute eyes and ears.

"It's a Richardson's shrew," she announced after looking it up in one of her zoology books, "and it's beneficial because it eats insects."

One cold day during a February weekend I walked in the snowy meadow beyond the ice rink, tracking a pheasant and a mink. The bird's track made two depressions much larger than his feet, and a sharp line was drawn between his foot-prints by his long, drooping tail. The mink track was easily identified because the spacing made it seem that the rear foot tracks were made by the front feet, a peculiarity to mink, I think. I was not uneasy for fear the mink had eaten the pheasant, for mink eat smaller things, such as frogs, fish, small birds, and rodents.

My rather lethargic tracking was stopped when I came

upon a snow mound about a foot high and three feet in diameter. For a while I stood studying it. Only one narrow path, about two inches wide, led into a small hole low on one side. I kicked the mound gently. It moved as one piece. Surprised, I stooped and lifted it on a side and glanced underneath. It broke into pieces then, and I saw it had been a fragile dome held by bent grasses iced together. On the ground beneath was an open burrow perhaps one and a half inches across. No droppings, no winter store of food, no bits of fur were there to give me the identity of the ingenious creature that had made this unusual windbreak-home.

"Maybe it was a meadow mouse," said Henry.

"They're awfully smart," said Virginia. "Such a large dome would fool a hawk or an owl. And a fox or a raccoon might go around it without suspecting it to be so fragile it could be broken with one blow of a paw."

Maybe so. Maybe not. It is still one of the many mysteries of nature that intrigue us as we explore.

Though as yet we have no beavers on our land, there are some east and west of us on the Wedde Creek, and two miles away on the Little Wedde they have become a menace to trout, damming the stream, thus slowing the flow and warming the water. They have cut tamaracks in Crandall Rogers' swamp and have threatened destruction of his new dam near the headwaters.

Henry thinks that beavers, while certainly extraordinary animals, are not infallible as loggers. He has found many, many trees they have cut and not used because, apparently, they were cut on the wrong side so that they fell in the wrong direction and were not then pulled to the place where the dam was to be built. I wonder whether the beavers may use the bark and twigs of these "wrong" trees for food while building their dam and home, thus making an asset of their mistake in logging. Or maybe they cut the trees on the wrong side on purpose; it seems to me that an animal showing such astonishing cleverness as to dam one or two streams in order to float logs to a third one would not make the mistake of cutting his logs on the wrong side.

Bill Doege told me of a beaver house ruined by the breaking of the big mill dam on the Frost Game Farm a half mile downstream from us. That house was found to have three levels and to be really complex in plan.

Since the young stay at home with their parents until three years old, a family may have as many as fifteen members living together. A large beaver weighs upward of seventy pounds and is about forty inches long. It is understandable, then, why the family residence must be sizable, perhaps fifteen feet across and three to five feet high.

"Beaver tail was eaten by the pioneers," Bill Doege told me. "Yes, sir, beaver tail was a real delicacy."

I wrinkled my nose. "I can't imagine myself eating such an efficient item!" I said.

"Well, beaver are protected nowadays," said he. "The tail ain't so smart either! Most folks believe the tail is like a trowel. Ain't so. They use their forepaws to mix the mud and sticks and stones, and they pull with their feet too. Their dams as well as their houses are made of this mud and small sticks, not big logs."

"Kind of a reinforced concrete?"

"You might call it that."

"What's the house like inside, Bill?"

"Oh, sort of channels and built-up places. The big 'room' is above water and has a sort of opening in the roof—for ventilatin', I guess."

"Why do you suppose beavers haven't come to our part of the stream? They're at Rogers'."

"You don't have a stand of poplars."

"Oh. Is that their favorite building material?"

"No. Food. Where there ain't popple, ain't beavers."

I considered that declaration, and when I returned to the farmhouse I looked up beaver in Seton's *Wild Animals I Have Known*. The author made the same statement, though more grammatically. I was particularly interested because the new section of stream we had just bought from Philip Sawin did have a clump of mature poplar, or aspen, with many young ones coming up. So, though we don't have a beaver dam and house, we expect to find them any spring.

Henry lamented an incident in his workshop: a little deer mouse fell into an open bucket of lubricating oil and drowned. Though much less abundant than the meadow mouse, deer mice are plentiful hereabout. They are slender gray mice, with tails as long as their bodies, seven inches overall. The tail is almost black above, but beneath it is pure white like the belly. No matter where on the farm we walk in snowtime, we see deer-mouse tracks, like those of sparrows except for the sharp, straight line made by the tail; they could be called pheasant tracks in miniature.

The reason Henry felt sad over the bad luck of one of these tiny creatures is that this mouse is a cunning friendly rodent, endearing itself to any who will take time to study its habits. Many's the time Henry has sat for an hour on a deer stand and watched a deer mouse investigate him. He crawls across Henry's boots and even halfway up his pants leg. Henry says that only the nuthatch equals the mouse in inquisitiveness.

One mouse built its globular nest in the vest pocket of an old coat of Henry's that he had left hanging in his workshop. Another built in a wood duck house waiting to be hung somewhere. That nest was eight inches across, but the one in the pocket was much smaller. Each nest was made of milkweed silk, bark, down from various plants, and grasses. The most ingenious feature was a self-closing side door! The nest was completely roofed over and was quite neat inside.

Their storage places are rarely near their nests, if our discoveries are typical. We found one food store in an ice-cream carton, one in a nail keg, and one in a brown paper sack that was half full of old handwrought spikes and nails. The stored food consisted of seeds, nuts, dried insects, and noxious weeds.

"I suppose he keeps these for emergencies," said Henry. "He doesn't hibernate. He searches for food all winter, the greedy little booger."

In late winter they pair off and raise four litters a season, three to five babies each time. I once surprised a mother as she was nursing her young; she ran off with all four hanging to her teats.

"I saw one carry a young one in her mouth as a cat does a kitten," Henry told me, "and as a squirrel does her little ones when moving to a new nest."

The predators of this mouse are the same as those of the meadow mouse—chipmunk, gopher, mole, rabbit, and all the other small mammals. Perhaps the marsh hawk, which nests on the ground and flies low over weeds and shrubs when searching for its food, is the worst enemy, though the great horned owl and diminutive saw-whet owl get their share, along with many other animals and birds for whom the various mice are staple food.

It has been said that the mouse was placed in the world for the salvation of better species. John Muir believed, on the other hand, that each animal was created for its own sake rather than many created for a few. At the same time, his philosophy that "everything is hitched to everything else" prevented his worrying about predation. This idea was subsequently popularized and practically applied to conservation by Aldo Leopold.

Henry and I feel that in nature every point has its counterpoint, every positive its negative—just as in the affairs of men things have a way of striking a general, if not an absolute, balance. So we do little about destroying predators, with the exception of starlings.

The Happy that I have been mentioning, the Happy that was sprayed by the skunk, was really our second dog by that name. The first one was a dignified male, affectionate and intelligent. Henry had selected him from a fine litter belonging to Dr. E. S. Elliott of Fox Lake, Wisconsin. Dr. Elliott called the pup "Professor." Because Henry's initials spelled HAP, I added the name Happy. The family name was Avono, so the registered dog was Avono Professor Happy. When he developed a carcinoma in one hind leg, and the veterinarian pronounced it eventually fatal, we took him to the farm for his last days.

When Henry, on a daily and nightly examination, found numerous lumps in Happy's chest and throat and head, he took him on his final hunt to his favorite quail area. When the dog smelled quail and painfully lifted his foot and pointed, Henry shot him in the head. Death was instantaneous. Henry dug his grave right there on the spot of the dog's final point, and we call it Happy's Happy Hunting Ground.

Henry ate no dinner afterward. Before we went to bed that night, he agreed that we'd return to Madison the next day by way of Fox Lake and try to get another Brittany spaniel as much like Happy as possible. All of Happy's pups were owned by people as fond of them as we had been of our dog, so we saw no probability of getting one of those.

Dr. Elliott let Henry have a frisky little male that resembled our Happy; we took him home with us that day, for he was eight weeks old. He was Happy the Second to us, though registered as Professor Happy Kaer. He grew into a perceptive hunter, successful in finding game, and tireless, but he had some bad habits; one was that he *would* chase rabbits. Henry tried several methods calculated to break the habit. None worked.

At Wichner's Store, Emil Wiesjahn told Henry that the smell of dead rabbit would cure the dog. In desperation, Henry shot a full-grown bunny and tied it around Happy's neck.

When they got out of the car at the farm, it was hard for me to decide which looked more embarrassed, Henry or the dog.

"I just have to do it," Henry apologized to both me and Happy. "He even left a point today to chase a cottontail. First time a dog of mine ever did that!"

He took Happy on his leash to the pen and left him without a word or a kind look. Happy slunk into the frame house, and we heard no sound from him.

We went to the kitchen and ate supper, not the rabbit stew I had prepared, but some hastily opened corned beef hash.

About an hour later Henry went out to see how Happy was taking his punishment. I walked with him as far as the gate and waited while he went into the dog's house.

He came out with disbelief on his face.

"He *ate* the whole dang thing! Hide, hair, bones—everything!"

I collapsed with laughter.

That was Happy all over, always doing the unexpected. We loved that dog, but we soon realized he would never be as satisfactory at hunting as his predecessor. During his first year, when Henry was too busy to pay him much attention, and the pen had Virginia's hens, we gave him the run of the farm and he took to hunting on his own. As a consequence, he never learned to stop when his master was ready to quit. He continued hunting alone.

During the second season Henry tied a fifty-foot length of window-sash cord to Happy's collar and tried hunting pheasants. The cord got tangled among cornstalks and threw Henry. This sort of outing was punishment for the man, not the dog; to Happy it was just another fun game.

Henry put up with him for still another season because all of us hated to part with him. Fast and vigorous, an excellent retriever, unafraid of water, he nevertheless was not fulfilling Henry's purpose in owning him. At last, when one of his pups was available to us, Henry decided to give Happy to a little girl we had grown fond of, Carolyn Harley. She and the dog already loved each other, and the transition was made with such evident pleasure on Happy's part that it was downright unflattering to us. Though he smiled whenever we went over to see him—he was the only dog we ever had that could really smile—after the first few minutes his eyes were for Carolyn alone.

His pup we named Skipper, registered as Avono Professor Skipkaer. He is more like the first Happy because his early training was approximately the same. He has known from the first that he is Henry's dog, not mine or Virginia's. He loves being at the farm, but he remains in his large pen except when Henry takes him out for grouse or quail or woodcock, or just to walk with him and let him enjoy the delicious smells of hill and shadowy valley.

Virginia's only objection to her Trig was that he could never bear or father a foal. She read many horse books, some of which had to do with breeding and with raising colts.

"We have such a lovely pasture for a colt," she said with a sigh.

"Maybe Mary Ellen's filly, Princess, will have a colt next spring, and you can help care for it." I knew that Wilma Baxter had had the filly bred, thinking that motherhood would calm her somewhat and make her a better riding horse for the four Baxter children.

They were another Madison family that had come to the area, buying a worn-out farm down on JJ. Mary Ellen, the eldest child, rode often with Virginia, but Virginia always returned with tales of how hard it was to manage pretty Princess. Even Mary Ellen said she was a "stubborn, independent *thing*." Ken, just younger, could handle her fairly well, but the two youngest could not ride her at all, and Wilma was afraid for them.

When running free in a pasture, Princess, a bay with four white feet, held her head high, but when riding on the road with Trig, she held her head in, with one eye always on him, and several times she bit him.

I had not seen her all winter. In February Wilma told me that she did not think the filly was in foal; her farmer neighbor, Ed Mueller, who took care of the mare, thought she had a hay-belly from overeating during the long winter in his barn. I compared her with Trig, who also had spent the time in a barn, Leo Schroeder's.

"She looks larger than Trig," I said, "but who am I, a mere city slicker, to doubt Ed's word?"

However, when Ken rode her over in May, she was still large.

"Ken, I think Princess is going to have a foal. Do you have things ready, just in case?"

"No," Ken said. "We think Ed Mueller ought to know horses pretty well; he's had plenty. Ed thinks Princess might have worms, and I'm going to Coloma now to get some worm medicine. Can Virginia go too?"

He rode her to Coloma and gave her the medicine when they reached their farm, and early that night Princess dropped one of the prettiest little colts I've ever seen!

Wilma was as excited as the children—more so, I think, for after they were asleep she went back to the barn and remained all night, working at making the stall more comfortable for the mare and colt. Ken, Sr., was out of the state on a scientific trip, so all responsibility rested on her.

Princess seemed nonchalant about the newcomer, but Wilma thought it was the normal way for the mare to act during the first hours.

At midmorning Ken had run to Ed's to tell him the news.

"Mr. Ed, Princess dropped a foal!"

"How's that?"

"Sure thing. Princess has a colt. A beauty too!"

Ed stood gaping, then coughed. "Er, I was a-tellin' my missus just yesterdy, 'That Baxter filly's goin' to foal.' Yes, sir, that's what I said, just yesterdy."

"Mom's a little worried 'cause Princess won't nurse the little one. She said to ask you what to do."

"Hmm-m. Mare'll know when to let her young-un nurse."

But when Virginia and I were there at noon, the colt was sucking Wilma's fingers, obviously very hungry. Princess would have nothing to do with him, and once she kicked him when he nosed her hard.

"There's a vet in Westfield," said Virginia hopefully.

Wilma telephoned him at once. He gave her a formula to prepare and told her how often to feed the colt; he urged that she continue her effort to get the mother to accept her foal, for the cholesterol in her milk was necessary for his survival.

We went again to the Baxters' in the afternoon and found Wilma really uneasy; the colt had eaten a little of the formula but hadn't relished it, and seemed weaker rather than stronger. Princess was openly hostile.

The children moved quietly and spoke softly, peeking at the colt through cracks in the wall instead of showing themselves, hoping the mare would become more tractable if not excited by them.

Ed came over but was not encouraging.

"Cain't no colt live lessen it git mare's milk," he declared. "I tried. George Semrow tried, Milford Carpenter, ole Emil Danner—none of us git one to live lessen its mother takes it."

That night Wilma slept a few hours, then at midnight she mixed a fresh batch and fed the colt.

We went over early the next morning, taking a pot of soup and a cake for the family.

"He didn't even raise his head this morning," said Wilma in a tearful voice.

The veterinarian came. When he saw that the mare did not even try to avoid stepping on the little one he said she might as well be put into another stall.

That done, Wilma stayed with the colt continuously, giving it a spoonful of formula again and again, and water also by the spoonful. But her care and concern were of no avail. With its head in her lap, the beautiful little animal died.

# VII   *A Song on the Wind*

T H E term "wildlife habitat" most assuredly includes birds. To me they are more important than the animals; with Henry they take second place, although he devotes almost as much time to their habitat improvement as he does to that for trout; to Virginia, whose primary interest in nature finally focused on the *behavior* of all living creatures, they are of equal importance and significance with animals.

As both Madison and Richford are in the natural flyway for bird migration, we get a great variety of birds that move

on farther north for nesting. All of us enjoy them while they
are with us, and we try to supply their favorite foods while
they are around. We find we can prolong their stay sometimes and even persuade a few to nest at Triple Ridge.

In September and October, when the southward trek begins, we keep the wire-mesh holders filled with suet and
Henry's feeders well supplied with sunflower seeds. They,
with the dried crab apples that have remained on the trees
and the luscious berries decorating the cranberry bushes,
persuade purple finches to stay with us. Cardinals and cedar
waxwings, too, remain when there is enough food. With
these birds the proximity of winter food is of more importance than the danger of below-zero weather.

Our winter residents are downy and hairy woodpeckers,
bluejay, belted kingfisher, white-breasted nuthatch, chick-
adee, tree sparrow, common redpoll, common snow bunting,
slate-colored junco, goldfinch, pine siskin, purple finch, tufted
titmouse and red-breasted nuthatch in mild winters, winter
wren, cedar and Bohemian waxwings, and the following
owls: short-eared, long-eared, barn, barred, snowy (rare),
great horned, and screech. English sparrows and starlings do
not like our woods in winter; they prefer residential areas.
The game birds remain all winter: ruffed grouse, pheasant,
quail, and occasionally woodcock. Darrell sees mallards
along the stream throughout the year.

In view of the fact that many insects and reptiles common
to some other sections of the United States do not survive in
Wisconsin, one might wonder why we have so many owls
and flycatchers and other insect-eating birds. We have no
ticks or chiggers at the farm, no poisonous snakes or spiders
or scorpions, no tarantulas, no termites. But we have plenty
of ants for the flickers, plant lice and aphids, grubs, red
spiders and ordinary spiders, wasps, bees, hornets, yellow

jackets, gnats, lightning bugs (the meadows are alight with them on summer nights, and their reflections in the swimming pool double the twinkling), caterpillars, and even a few crayfish and fresh-water clams for water or shore birds to feast on.

In the bogs are earthworms, which are the chief food of the interesting woodcock. As Bill Doege would say, "Where there ain't no worms, ain't no woodcock." On our farm this bird is not abundant as yet; perhaps I'd better say we haven't seen many of them. It is a quiet bird and we can miss him entirely unless he is flushed by Skipper. He remains in the autumn until he can no longer dig his worms out of the frozen sand; then he flies south to remain until the frost is out of the ground in March, when he returns to the North to breed.

"I can take you to a woodcock hideout," said Henry one day when I had wondered why I so seldom saw one.

He led me through a hummocky marsh near the guest cottage, a section of young poplar, alder, willow, and a few scattered jack pines, with open damp sand a few feet away. In the sand were many round holes made by the bird's highly specialized bill, a remarkably flexible instrument; the outer end of the upper mandible can be flipped outward and inserted into the ground for a depth of three inches!

"I watched a woodcock one day when I was resting on the opposite bank of the stream," said Henry. "Every time he inserted his bill he drew out a worm! I suppose he locates them through a sense of smell or maybe hearing. He often held his ear to the ground."

We both wore rubber boots that day so we could maneuver among the many springs and bogs of the area. I carried a folded bag in a pocket of my jacket, for, though it was only April, I hoped to find a new early flower to take back to the herbarium. The only blossom I saw was the familiar waxy yellow ranunculus, but this one was just about perfect; so, though I had already collected a specimen, I stooped to pick it. But I didn't even touch it, for beside it lay four buffy eggs sprinkled with little brown spots.

"Oh, Henry, look!"

"That's woodcock all right," he said. "I've seen only one other, and it looked just like that, hardly a nest at all, just a depression near a spring." He stooped and lifted a dried sprig of last year's bracken, with which the nest seemed to be lined.

"How perfectly camouflaged it is," I said.

"Like the woodcock himself, brown and beige. There could be dozens of birds around, but we'd not see them unless they zigzagged off from under our feet."

We didn't linger, for we wanted the female to return to her eggs.

Leopold, in his *Sand County Almanac*, describes this bird's courtship flight, which occurs just when I am starting dinner in the spring, just after sunset; otherwise I'd often be on hand to watch it. Leopold calls it the sky dance, for the male loops and spirals and flutters, *peenting* and twittering, and then at the climax he "tumbles like a crippled plane, giving voice in a soft liquid warble that a March bluebird might envy."

One evening two males were performing at the same time about one hundred yards apart. Each bird beeped like a satellite every third second, the two sometimes in concert, sometimes alternately. Their faint wing music had to be listened for intently as other evening music was more audible. After I heard the soft twittering I knew the birds were going to drop earthward; I concentrated on the one nearer to me. A soft warble, and then in a breath he was down. The beeping began again almost immediately, and perhaps five or six minutes later the sky dance was repeated.

Quail nests are as numerous at Triple Ridge as woodcock nests are scarce. We have found the domed twiggy nests of quail in a variety of places. The first one gave me the biggest thrill. One Sunday afternoon in late May, shortly after we had bought the farm, I slipped off alone for a last look at the newly cleaned Birch Spring before we should leave for Madison. I walked halfway up the steep hill above the spring to get a total view of the valley. A quail startled me as she flushed from the base of an oak only three or four feet from me. Leaves, dried grasses, and twigs formed a rounded hut with an opening low on the east side, through which I could see nine white eggs. I knelt there for a minute, noting that the eggs were pointed on one end and that the nest looked liked an overturned gallon-sized basket. I ran back to the house then and joyfully told Henry, Virginia, and Gretchen Ihde about it. All of us went to see it, hoping the hen had not returned, for we wouldn't want to frighten her a second time.

"I'm glad they're going to breed here," said Henry as we climbed the hill. That being our first season, he had wondered about the permanence of our quail.

Each of us knelt in turn to peer and to exclaim.

Later that year and the next we came upon nests in the wild grape vines along the north fence and among the red pines on Warren Knob, as we call that plantation toward the old Warren farm. One August we frightened a bird off her nest in tall grass, but, though Henry and I searched carefully, we could not find it, so well hidden it was. A month later, after rain had beaten down the grass, we saw it, still containing the shells left by thirteen young birds.

Last June I stopped to smell a crab-apple blossom by the bridge pool. A quail astonished me by rising from between my feet! Thinking I might be standing over her nest, I stepped wide to avoid it. Then I stood very still and searched with my eyes for eggs or for a rounded effect in the grass that might be a nest. I could see none. That night I told Henry about it before we went to sleep.

"I was petrified!" I said. "But I couldn't for the life of me find her nest."

"I bet it was there," said he. "I'll look for it in the morning."

He found it a few inches away from the young crab apple, the eggs hidden beneath grass that was bent and twisted in such a natural way that I had not suspected it. Eleven birds came from the nest in late August.

We are fond of this little bird, so articulate and friendly he is. We whistle him up to our porch, near which we have strewn corn and buckwheat. He walks up, wary but eager, and ever so attractive in his black-and-white-striped cap. We whistle inexpertly, and he answers readily as if he didn't hear our off-notes. Through the raspberries in the Wildwood he struts, or he flies in from a low limb of a pine to the golden feast laid out for him.

It is natural for human beings to like best those birds and animals we can "do for." We can help quail survive the cruel winters by making available to him man-made shelters such as the open implement shed and the log house; we can see that food is available during the deep snows. Whereas the woodcock, quiet and secretive and self-sufficient, will have none of us; when a condition beyond our control (the freezing of his worm bog) displeases him, he moves on.

As we grew in awareness, we found more and more bird nests. That of the ruby-throated hummingbird was as interesting as any. Virginia stooped one day to pluck a wild pasture rose. A mother hummingbird whirred from her nest beside Virginia's face, just thirty inches from the ground. Virginia paused long enough to see that this one had two tiny eggs and that it was built on a stout twig about halfway along the oak limb. Then she came running for me.

"Hurry before the mother returns," she said. "This might be the only opportunity you'll ever have to look into her nest." Ten feet from the ground is the usual height of this one-and-a-half-inch nest.

The eggs were about the size of a big pearl, perhaps three-eighths of an inch in diameter. We refrained from touching the gray-lichen-and-spider-web structure with its lining of plant down, thinking we'd examine it after the young birds had flown.

Each weekend we visited the nest to watch the growth of one little bird that hatched. I don't know what finally became of the second egg. It remained in the nest for several days, long enough for us to know it would not produce another fledgling. Then one day the little bird seemed to have only his feet and tummy inside the nest. His tail, what there was of it, stuck out on one side, his head out the other, and his wings overflowed the whole. We took a good long look this time, for we knew he'd be gone before we could come again. He did not yet have the brilliant throat, but there was a little green in his gray wings and back, and his underside was almost white. He sat very still while we discussed him, our faces only a foot away.

The next week he had flown, and Virginia cut off the oak limb on which the nest was saddled so she could show it to the students in one of her classes. I later took it to my home-town, Nacogdoches, and placed it in a case in the Old Stone Fort Museum. The same species of hummingbird breeds in that area, and it is not improbable that our little builder spends her winters in that historic town.

The Wayne Moores have a hummingbird nest on an oak limb near the door of their summer cottage. The same nest has been used annually for several years. Our conclusion is that, though this is the softest kind of nest we know about, it is not fragile.

There is no need for us to put out vials of sugar water to attract these fleet birds; the great supply of funnel-shaped wild flowers in meadow and rock garden furnishes plenty of nectar. Among the cultivated flowers in the buildings area are plantain lily, day lilies, campanula, thermopsis, and coral bells—all of which the hummingbirds like. I watch them through the binoculars, and I've seen them rest for as long as five minutes on dead oak branches ten to fifteen feet above the ground. Then they fly off again to thrust their long black bills down fragrant tubes, furiously beating their gauzelike wings to hold their bodies in steady suspension.

"They're treading air," said Fritz, "like midget helicop-ters."

One day when I was at the Audubon Camp in Sarona, a ruby-throat, getting nectar from a flowering apple tree, swung away and into the windshield of a parked car. Though sorry to witness the death of so lively and colorful a creature, I was able to learn about him in a way that would have been impossible while he was alive. At death, one of his tongues, or one part of the double-hinged tongue—which-ever it is—protruded three-quarters of an inch from the tip of the bill. It was not as firm to the touch as the bill but was certainly harder than a human tongue. The second tongue, or part, remained inside the bill. Possibly the bird thrusts one section at a time into a tubular blossom; having two, he wastes no time. Perhaps with the second part he picks off an aphid or a mosquito, for he consumes small insects as well as the drop of juice in a flower.

One of our spring privileges is to save the song sparrow from the lazy parasitic cowbird. We consciously interfere with nature in this undertaking and have no regret. Armed with silver teaspoons and wearing short boots or rubber sandals to protect our feet from the rough gravel and stones, we take to the stream. We quietly search the banks for song sparrow nests, laying back the grass with gloved hands. When we find a nest, we look at each egg. If all are small, greenish-white, and splotched with brown, we do not meddle. But if one is larger than the others and is white, evenly speckled with brown, we lift it out with the spoon.

"Now neither Mama nor Papa Sparrow will be the wiser," I remark as the cowbird egg is cast away, "and our farmland will profit more without the lazy progeny."

Robins and catbirds will throw out these eggs, recognizing them as fakes among the blue eggs of the robin and glossy blue-green eggs of the catbird, but we suspect that the coloration is too much like her own for the mother sparrow to detect the fraud. The result is that the song sparrow sits on the big egg until it hatches. Then the strong foster child knocks the smaller eggs from the nest. The sparrows work themselves to exhaustion trying to bring enough food for this strange child. Out of pity we take a hand as soon as Henry reports in May that the sparrow eggs are being laid.

The song sparrow is easily identified. Both sexes are

streaked all over, and on the breast is a dark center spot. His song is a happy one of seven to eleven notes, and it is usually delivered from a fallen branch near the stream or in the fen meadow, where he can find wee bugs in the leaves and sphagnum moss. He is one of the many birds that use some of Trig's hair in the construction of their nests. When the horse rubs against rough bark to rid himself of his heavy winter coat, he leaves bunches of hair, and the birds tug at it until they get enough.

One day I was awakened from a catnap in the hammock by a meowing in the blackberry bushes. Henry had told me of seeing a big cat in the swamp, but it was not a cat that came from the bushes and perched on the stump to which the hammock was attached; it was a catbird, and he was not frightened. He preened himself contentedly for a few minutes, then he dropped to the ground to pick up a long straw and returned to the blackberries. He hopped through them to the Tartarian honeysuckle, and then I heard more meowing and some scratching sounds. Two birds were working together; they were building a nest eight feet from my hammock.

"I hope you're the lovers I saw on the white-oak limb," I said to them. "I'll be able to see your babies grow up."

Eggs were laid in time, four blue-green ones that shone as if waxed and polished. I peeked just once.

When they were about two weeks old, while I was working in the kitchen, I heard a sudden loud scolding followed by many sharp snapping notes with screeching. I ran out, vegetable brush in hand. The honeysuckle was swaying violently. Two gray squirrels jumped from it to the stump and then into the nearest oak, the two catbirds darting at their heads. The squirrels ran and jumped along their aerial trail through the Wildwood and across the driveway into the pines. As long as I watched, the catbirds attacked them.

I walked down to the honeysuckle to investigate. The nest was intact but empty of its bright treasures.

Red-headed woodpeckers, like rabbits and skunks, move slowly when crossing roads and are therefore frequent victims of cars. In some regions the red-heads are, I believe, becoming scarce, but at our farm this amusing and colorful bird is in numbers of from eight to twenty per season. A very noisy bird in both juvenile and adult stages, the red-head attracts attention to his activities and is easy to follow about. He may play shy at first, hopping to the back side of pole or post or tree trunk when he sees you, but soon he comes out so you can admire him. He doesn't remain all winter as regularly as his cousins, the downy and hairy, but occasionally he does. In January I have watched him find an acorn lodged in the crotch of an oak. He cracks it and eats it. Apparently the diet is more varied than that of the two others I mentioned, but not more so than that of our other three woodpeckers—the red-bellied, the flicker, and the rare pileated.

Of the six, however, the red-headed is, without a doubt, the most patient parent. I have seen a mother try to teach her stupid baby how to find food for himself. She finds an insect halfway up an oak and calls to her young one in a not unpleasant voice. The young may be fifty feet away sitting hunched on a limb. If he does not respond at all, she uses a rather harsh call and pecks hard on the bark a few inches away from the insect, which she has dazed with a blow. The young may raise his head and look lazily in her direction.

She scolds and raps harder. If he doesn't fly to her, she flies to him and pushes him off his secure seat. He flaps awkwardly to the ground. She hops along in front of him for a few feet, then she scolds again until he follows her to the base of the tree that contains his dinner.

She persuades him to start up the tree. He goes up several inches and stops. She pushes him with her bill. Finally he is almost at the spot where the insect is. The mother picks up the fly (or grub or beetle) and puts it nearer her beloved. She goes below him and shoves him closer. At last, when he has only to open his bill, the young woodpecker gobbles his food. The mother fairly prances with pride. This goes on day after day until we marvel at the faith of woodpecker motherhood.

Another of the commonest and tamest birds on our land, indeed in all the Richford area, is the phoebe. Having so many open sheds with rafters and eaves and window ledges, this tidy gray bird needs no aid from us for shelter, and as its food is flying insects, we welcome it.

"The phoebe has beaten us to the farm again this year," Henry called from the yard while we were unpacking for our Easter vacation.

"Time for her to nest," I said.

I recalled our watching three adult phoebes come one year to help two parents feed their five babies for two days when they were about ready to leave their nest. We have not seen this happen again, nor have we heard of another authentic case, but we are sure about this particular one.

The nest was on the top ledge of a window six feet from our porch, so that we could sit there and observe. The young were so large that we thought they would soon be falling out if not persuaded out. Their mouths were nearly always open. When an insect was brought by the parents, all five mouths begged, and four squawked protestingly while the lucky one swallowed the morsel with the help of his parent, who bit it into small pieces and pushed each piece down the throat of the one she had chosen to feed.

"Look," said Henry one morning, "there are five elders sitting together now. Where did the three new ones come from?"

There were indeed five mature birds sitting on the edge of the roof. Two of them flew away toward the pond and brought back insects. While they were feeding the young ones, two more adults flew toward the meadow and brought back food, the fifth waiting till their return before flying away. The first two rested on the electric wire a few feet away until the fifth came back. Then the whole procedure was repeated all through that day and the next.

Toward evening of the second day the expected happened; during joyful activity in the nest, one young bird lost his place and toppled over the side. As he clung to the bottom, fluttering and frightened, Henry jumped out of his chair and ran around the corner of the house, returning in a minute with a short stepladder, which he placed beneath the nest. Hardly waiting to make sure the ladder was steady, he climbed it and cupped his hand under the little bird. It immediately let go and snuggled into his palm.

"Doesn't resemble his neat parents very much," he said as Virginia and I stood close to look at him. "He's just plain sloppy, as a matter of fact."

"He'll soon lose his yellow bill," said Virginia.

"And he'll be as well-groomed as his parents," I added, "after he has learned how to preen. He has two wing bars now, but he'll lose those, too, won't he, as his feathers mature?"

Henry set the fledgling in a honeysuckle bush near the nest so it would be in sight of the parents.

"That's a good place," said Virginia, "for when the other babies fall out or fly out, they'll probably drop into that bush with him."

The five adults had watched Henry from the moment he had appeared with the ladder. Sitting a few inches apart on the wire, they made no move toward the little one while we were in sight. We went indoors and tried to see without being seen, but soon it was dark, and we had to wait until morning.

During the night a storm raged for an hour. I lay sleepless in the noisy darkness and feared the little bird would drown. But when it was light and the air cheerful with the cheeping of busy birds, I went to the porch and peered into the bush and around it on the ground. At last I spied him in a wild cherry tree, as pert a youngster as I ever did see. He was higher than the nest; so we knew he had exercised his own wings to get there.

With the removal of the first baby from the nest the three helpers left, thinking, I suppose, the parents would be able to handle the situation thereafter. Three of the young left the nest the next day, but the last one, probably exulting in the unaccustomed privacy and room to stretch in, remained alone until he realized his parents were too busy with the other four, sitting on a high electric wire at the edge of the meadow, to return to him often enough to satisfy his hunger. He then awkwardly balanced himself on the edge of his erstwhile home and flew in brief jaunts to join them.

It was amusing to watch the young ones develop courage to catch their own food. The adults worked closely, making short sallies into clouds of insects; the young ones imitated, sometimes successfully, but often not. By noon they were leaving the wire more readily and venturing farther afield.

I think that of all the bird families we have watched we enjoyed this one the most.

Two English sparrows furnished fun for Virginia when she was still in high school. Ray White told her that sparrows could be finger-trained, like parakeets. So when we decided to remove a sparrow nest from a bluebird house and found that two of the eggs had already hatched, Virginia adopted the babies, and ugly featherless little things they were. Carefully she made a bed in a shoe box, using cotton batting she had "borrowed" from a sofa pillow. On the way to Madison that Sunday afternoon she fed them with bits of earthworm on a toothpick.

They had to be fed every hour of the day, she said. At night she set her alarm clock for three feedings. Guess who fed them the worms next day while she was in school. And guess who had to cut up more worms before she returned in the afternoon. Ugh!

Well, those two birds survived, and they did learn to hop to her finger whenever she put it into the canary cage to which they had been transferred. She whistled a strange little tune to them, which they recognized and to which they responded. After they had flown around her room for a little while, she whistled, and they came to her and allowed her to return them to the cage.

"I'll release them," she promised, "as soon as they can drink from a saucer. Then I'll know they can drink from the pond and stream."

Their diet had progressed to mash. When they could eat

seeds from the floor of the cage, she took them to the farm to let them go.

"I'll open a window and set the cage on the sill. Then I'll open their door. I think they'll leave but come back to the cage for the night."

That's exactly the way it happened. She brought them inside at twilight but set them out again the next day after they had eaten a good breakfast. This time she hung the open cage against a wall of the house, on Henry's deer antlers. The birds flew to an oak. Several times that morning she held up a finger and whistled. One of them flew to her each time, but the other one stayed in the tree, disappearing altogether after his first night out. The tamer one stayed in the area all weekend, but when Virginia was ready to leave Sunday afternoon she whistled in vain.

"He's gone," she sighed. "But my experiment was a success. One *can* finger-train an English sparrow."

In the deepest woodland on the farm one cold windy day in May I found the nest of a hermit thrush in a swale. Well concealed by skunk-cabbage leaves and last year's pearly everlasting, it was built of moss and grass and leaves, and it lay flat on the ground. That night a hard frost came, coating with ice the red partridge berries and last August's seed of rattlesnake orchid near the nest. That being the only hermit nest I had ever seen, I very much wanted to help this pair of thrush survive; accordingly I took some chopped apple, orange, banana, and some millet seed and went early to the low spot to spread the food around on the frozen ground.

Other thrush are visible in the spring: the veery is often in the basswoods along the stream, the wood thrush among the tall oaks and birches, and the brown thrasher, commonly called the brown thrush around Richford, in the hawthorn by the swimming pool, in the brush pile by the garden, and in the wild-plum thickets along the road and driveway.

Nearly a foot long, this red-brown thrasher with heavily streaked breast attracts attention by the lusty way it throws dead leaves aside with its bill and then scratches for insects. The wood thrush has the same habit of feeding among dead leaves, but it is four inches shorter, and on its sides are spots instead of streaks. Too, it is not usually seen in the sunny, brushy places chosen by the thrasher.

"The wood and hermit thrush sound like flutes," said Virginia, "but the thrasher is rather harsh at times."

"Sometimes, yes," I agreed, "but one day when I was clearing a picnic spot in the oaks on Pine Ridge I heard a beautiful song coming from the top of a thirty-foot oak. It was loud and rich and very melodious. I stopped pruning and raking to listen. It was so lovely that I lost all sense of time. That was a thrasher. He warbled and trilled and seemed to be singing, 'Pretty girl, pretty girl, pretty girl, come here, come here, hello, hello, hello, trill . . .' I'd never really heard a thrasher's song before that day."

"I sometimes have trouble identifying a veery," said Virginia.

"I, too, because he also is a brown bird, but he has a pale breast. At least the spots are so pale they don't show much. His song is pretty, but it sounds remote to me even when he isn't far away. His voice is more like a harp than a flute, and his song is a series of notes, each lower in pitch than the preceding one."

All the thrushes like berries and seed, and the thrasher also likes acorns and buckwheat, so in times of stress we are able to help them; whereas the insect eaters, like the wood pewee and the phoebe, are pretty much on their own at all times.

Ray and Alden discovered a bobolink in our alfalfa field near the garden. To see this stylish black and white male wearing his trim beige hood gives me a special thrill, for he takes me back to my childhood when I recited "Bob-o-link, Bob-o-link, spink, spank, spink . . ." and never expected actually to see one of the birds swaying on a meadowsweet bush or to hear his bubbly song. Each spring this is now my privilege. On two occasions, however, tragedy struck the bobolink family. The field was mowed early, ruining the nest before the eggs had hatched. Since there is but one brood per season, the whole long journey from Paraguay or northern Argentina had been made in vain. Since then I have tried to find the flimsy nest in the tallest alfalfa and place a stake near it to warn Henry.

The cedar and Bohemian waxwings, our only brown songbirds with crests, sometimes nest in the Wildwood cedars, pines, and oaks. As their chief food is fruit, I habitually identified them in my mind with the crab apples and plums growing in what used to be the Wentlands' orchard. But last summer I was able to concentrate on them more than usual, and I found that they also eat the berries of juniper, rose hips, hawthorn apples, mountain-ash berries, and cherries. In midsummer they came in flocks of fifty or sixty to the birches around Birch Pond and caught as many insects over the water as did the flycatchers.

But one incident in August has made me think of chokecherries whenever the waxwing is mentioned or seen. Our Madison pastor, the Reverend Dr. Alfred Swan, and his wife, Eva, were our guests for a few days. From the screened porch we watched a mother waxwing feed her two babies, which were sitting on one of the willow logs I had laid at the edge of the lilies of the valley. The feeding went on for an hour. We went to the kitchen for our lunch and returned to the porch at one o'clock to stretch out in the hammock and glider. The little birds were still in the same spot. At three o'clock they were still on the same log and the mother still busy bringing food.

"The first day out of the nest," I told the Swans, "the little ones are not afraid of human beings. They seem to think that everything approaching them has good intentions. I could feed them."

Dr. Swan expressed surprise. "Do you think you could— now? Give one a cherry perhaps?"

"I can try." I laughed.

With that he and I walked out and slowly approached the baby birds, Dr. Swan getting his camera ready. One of the birds hopped to a stub that stuck up about two feet just below a chokecherry tree. He looked at me but made no move to jump off.

I reached up and pulled off a cherry, stoned it quickly, and held it just above the bird's head. He opened his beak wide and I dropped it in. He swallowed. Dr. Swan got the picture. I gave the bird three cherries, my fingers within an inch of his mouth every time.

The next morning both birds had left the log but were only a few feet away among some pink turtlehead and false Solomon's-seal. I gave a cherry to one of them as he sat on the ground.

As I have said before, we seldom interfere between pre-dator and victim, for we realize there must be a balance. Field mice would soon own the farm were it not for the raptors, hawks and great horned owls; ants might be a real menace were it not for flickers; there might even be too many cute chipmunks were there no weasels or red fox.

We have seen many a fight and many a victory and have come to feel more tender toward certain animals and birds than toward others, but there are few that we have tried to destroy. Among these are the starling and the destructive yellow-bellied sapsucker. The latter was riddling our young pines with small holes. We thought he was after grubs like the woodpeckers, but when we examined a dead one, we found he had a tongue that was a good deal like a brush. He had made the holes so the sap would bleed and he could then lap it up. The sap attracted insects, which he joyously devoured, and he seemed also to pull out tiny strips of inner bark, which is said to be nutritious.

We scared him away from the trees near the house, and I even resorted to sticks and stones. Nowadays he doesn't stay around the buildings; he goes into deeper woods—if he is there at all. We seldom see him.

On three occasions I have seen starlings kill bluebirds and then take over the houses the bluebirds were trying to nest in.

"Henry, I wish you'd shoot those starlings! They really get my dander up!" I complained to him.

"They're listed as songbirds, you know," he said, taking down his .22.

"They don't sing for me. We work so hard to encourage the bluebirds and then have to sit quietly by and watch these dirty squawking starlings kill them!"

When they get too numerous, Henry shoots two of them and hangs the dead birds over an electric light wire. That scares the rest of them away. After three or four days he removes the dead ones. I am told that the same method is used with unwanted grackle, but we haven't had them at the farm.

When we find the starlings' dirty nesting-trees in the woods, we destroy the nests and young; the trees are easily found, for they are splashed with the gray and white droppings the adults throw out of the nests.

To Ira's birdhouses Henry has added many more, using slabs, gourds, and boards, even short logs. He makes holes in them according to the size needed by the specific birds he hopes will find and use the boxes, for instance:

| | |
|---|---|
| 1 inch | wren |
| 1 1/4 inch | nuthatch |
| 1 1/2 inch | bluebirds, tree swallows, chickadees |
| 2 inches | red-headed woodpecker |
| 2 1/2 inches | several holes in a big house for martins |
| 3 inches | small owls |
| 3 by 4 inches | wood ducks |

One day while I was weeding *baptisia* and *platycodon* in the flower border, an unfamiliar car came up the driveway. I nodded at the stranger but moved nearer the house. He stopped in the parking area and walked toward me, smiling. He was obviously a city man, for he wore stylish casual slacks and suede jacket.

"I am Walter Thompson, a member of a wood-duck association," he introduced himself. "I am looking for likely places in which to hang wood-duck houses. You seem to have an ideal habitat for them—a long valley with a stream through it and woods along the hillside. Would you accept two wood-duck boxes and hang them according to instructions?"

"Why, of course! We'd be delighted to have them."

He went back to his car and removed two cylindrical boxes, each about a yard high with an entry hole two-thirds of the way up. The interior was at least eight inches square and as high as the exterior of the box. The roof was conical to discourage predators.

"They should be hung with the opening to the east or southeast," he told me, "and the bottom is ideally about ten feet from the ground to make it safe from fox and weasel. The tree must be free of limbs within a radius of eight feet of the nest so the archenemy, the squirrel, can't jump into the box."

"I promise to follow your instructions to the letter, and thank you very much." As he entered his car, I called to him, "May we place more than two in our valley—if my husband wants to make some more like these?"

"Oh yes. You might put one or two on poles standing in your stream."

And that's what Henry and Ira did. Ira made a duck house out of a hollow log, and he and Henry set it on a ten-foot pole in the shallow end of the swimming pool. Henry made one of boards and set it atop a pole downstream where an island has formed in a wide bend of the creek. In both locations the young will have only to drop out of their nests to reach water. The two ready-made nests were attached to maples in the valley; Henry first pruned away all branches according to the donor's instructions.

Wood ducks come each April to the swimming pool before the ice has entirely melted. From the kitchen we watch them swimming around the floe.

"Maybe they'll stay with us this time," I say hopefully.

"They're certainly the prettiest duck," says Henry, "and they strut even while they swim."

I know what he means. The beautiful crested head is held with dignity whether the bird is in the water or in the air.

We have plenty of food for the wood duck: watercress,

wild rice, duckweed, and seeds of sedges and grasses. So we hope that soon we shall have several families remaining with us each season, not to be hunted but to be enjoyed. At present a hunter is allowed to kill two wood ducks a day during the season. I sincerely hope this bird will soon be again on the protected list.

We have watched the broken-wing pantomime performed by quail, grouse and blue jay as well as by the meadow lark.

Once when a quail mother tried to attract my attention away from her brood by going through her act of fluttering off with one wing trailing as if injured, I saw her little ones freeze where they stood, one at the edge of my path. I couldn't resist picking him up in my gloved hands. Cuddling him, I thought how like a baby chicken he looked, so soft and downy. I glanced around for the mother, but she was so well camouflaged that I didn't find her, although I knew she was tensely watching me. I set the baby on the path and went my way.

My way that September day led to the bank where I had seen a patch of fringed gentians the year before. As they are biennials, I expected to find few at the same place but hoped to find many a little distance away. When I came upon the location, I found only two gentians in bloom and five in bud. Unless they are in blossom, they are hard to find, for the grass is often taller than they. I searched for fifteen feet around but found no more. As I was about to leave, a muskrat came out of his hole on the opposite bank, saw me, and quickly melted back into the darkness of his home. It was then that I saw the gentians. The wind had apparently blown seed across the water. Many were blooming, enough to make an area about five feet square of deep, deep blue, breathtaking in its intensity.

Suddenly I saw a spot of greener blue swinging on a meadowsweet. It was an indigo bunting. He'll be leaving us soon, I thought, lifting my binoculars to see whether his wing feathers had begun to turn brown. They had, and some of his breast feathers were quite pale. I searched the surrounding bushes for his mate and found her, demure and almost colorless, eating seeds. Earlier in the year they are insect eaters, but in the fall they eat many weed seeds. I wondered how brown the male would be by the time he reached his winter quarters in Cuba or Panama or southern Mexico.

Of the grosbeaks, the evening and rose-breasted are very welcome residents at Triple Ridge. Their color alone would make them desirable—bright yellow, and black and white with bright rose. Both eat insects when flies and mosquitoes are most numerous, and the evening grosbeak eats the seed of box elder.

Redwing blackbirds are among the first returning residents. Whenever we walk the stream banks after these birds have built their nests in the alders and *Spiraea tomentosa*, they flare in noisy explosions all around us. They are realistic birds. No pretension is in their make-up, and they are suspicious of us in April and May. Not until we are there for long periods do they trust us enough to come to our bird tree; in mid-June they fly to the feeder, pick up a seed, and fly away as if threatened with instant annihilation. In July they will linger awhile. In August they will sometimes stay at the feeder even if we are sitting on the terrace.

One June, after a difficult winter when snow had lain two feet deep for two months at a stretch, and the Big Thaw had come in April, only to be followed by another blizzard, we anxiously listened to the calling of two lonely cock pheasants. All the hens were gone, victims of either fox or weather.

After three weeks of pitying the two cocks we went to the State Game Farm and talked with Damaske.

"We are to plant pheasants on the state-owned land just downstream from you," he told us. "Your cocks will find plenty of hens in just about another week."

Two days later, when I was alone for an hour or so, a truck stopped in our driveway; two men got out and opened the rear door, took out a large cage, and opened it. Out flew a dozen pheasants, cocks and hens, all flying east at a rapid pace. I was standing where I could see them skim our long valley. It seemed to me that all of them flew to the state-owned property a quarter of a mile away. But next day when our cocks called, a young hen stepped onto the pool bank. Soon a cock found her, and they disappeared into the Wildwood. When I walked to the blueberry area, I saw our other cock and another hen together. That September we came upon two coveys of eleven birds each. The male pheasant is polygamous, so I am sure our two cocks were responsible for more than two coveys, though probably on other land.

The next spring we saw only six or seven adults. The winter had been an easy one, and the Fenskes had left some standing corn for the wildlife, but few pheasants were around. In July, Henry decided to cut the clover in the north field. He first walked around the field looking for bird nests. When he found none, he began to mow. Suddenly a young hen flew up just ahead of him. He was able to stop his tractor before he hit the nest. He brought the tractor back to the house, saying he'd rather lose the twenty dollars that the clover would bring than to ruin another nest.

Twice he returned to the field to see whether the hen had come back to her ten white eggs. She had not. Next morning he slipped up behind dogwood and ninebark until he could see the nest. She still had not returned to cover them, probably because they were now exposed to predators.

That fall we found only one covey. Last year we neither saw nor heard a pheasant all season. Central Wisconsin is at the northern edge of the area in which this bird thrives; we therefore cannot expect ever to find it in abundance.

"We don't seem to have the kind of grist they need," said Henry. "Our pheasants are hybrids of several races, but that should not be a factor when the ecology is right. We seem to have most of what they like: good winter cover, marsh and bog, young oaks and young conifers, ungrazed wood lots, plenty of grass and clover and alfalfa."

"And dock and dandelion," I added.

"Yes, and dried fruits and seeds. Of course, seeds are their most important food."

"I've seen them eating ragweed and wild-sunflower seed, even those of skunk cabbage, jewelweed, and the smartweeds on the pond bank. And I saw one jump for a grasshopper."

"I just don't know," said Henry. "Lack of the right kind of grist is all I can think of that would make them disappear like this. I've been leaving corn for them to eat in winter—I just don't know. Fox and owls couldn't make away with so many. Darrell says he shot only two last hunting season. I didn't shoot any. Of course, poachers may have got them."

"I think Darrell would have known if they had; he keeps pretty close watch on our place because of his trapping here."

The crow-size pileated woodpecker is another bird that does not thrive here despite the dense woodlands. Though I have found his feeding holes, three by four inches in size, in a few dying oaks in the densest part of our woods (he

searches out trees that are infested with carpenter ants),
and once found a nest of young pileateds in the Mittelstadt
woodland, this species is rare in Waushara County. According to Professor George Becker, it used to be fairly common
here but has moved north and west. I wonder whether the
cause is not the encroachment of residential and recreational
areas on what used to be wilderness. This bird prefers extensive forests. Our wooded sections are often small and
more often grazed. The severe cold cannot be the deterrent
factor, else this species would not be found at the Audubon
Camp in Sarona, which is a hundred miles north of Waushara County.

At this point in my rumination I am reminded that in
East Texas, which is more populated than our area, the
pileated woodpecker sometimes comes into backyards and
city parks. Indeed, one came to the yard of a friend of mine
in Nacogdoches and seemed so tame that my friend thought
the bird sick. He was easily caught by hand and was fed
some canary and parakeet seed. Then my friend took him to
the house, put him into a carton and placed a board across
the top. His intention was to tend the bird after his return
from church service that morning, but when he came home
he found no woodpecker. Instead, there was a three-inch
square hole in the wall of the house. With its extraordinarily
powerful bill, the bird had made the opening next to the
window frame.

Curtis Lake is only three miles from Triple Ridge. Pleasant, Wood, and Crystal Lakes are other water areas near us,
with Trout and Fish Lakes at Hancock, seven miles to the
north, Fish and Silver Lakes at Wautoma, and scattered
among these are many smaller ponds. Twenty lakes, as many

as there are trout streams, lie within a radius of ten miles of our farm. Most of the water and shore birds are to be found in the area, making it attractive to both amateur and professional bird watchers.

Though Triple Ridge Farm is only a small portion of this broad section, it offers more than enough opportunity for bird study. I am reminded of the bird "apartments" that developed one year between Henry's workshop and the granary. Ira Kurth's wren box had hung there for several years and had always been used by wrens. Last year, however, a robin built on *top* of the box before the wren came back. We expected a real fight, for wrens are particular about their homes, but apparently the two species solved their problem amicably; the wren built inside as usual, and baby robins were reared in their straw-and-mud penthouse. It happened again this year.

Henry set another wren box on the middle post of the section of fence running in front of our veranda; he went indoors for a drink of water, and when he returned to get the birdhouse a wren flew out of it. He hesitated about picking it up and was astonished when a second wren entered it with a twig. She flew almost under his outstretched hand.

"Ruth," he called, "come see our new pets. What should I do?"

I watched for a few minutes, and both of us laughed at the antics of these busy creatures. They brought rather heavy twigs, sometimes too large to go through the small opening. In that case the bird dropped the twig and picked it up at a different spot so the angle would be different. Often the twig then went into the box, but once the bird repeated that maneuver three times before he held it so that it went through the opening.

"Let's see what they will do during the night," I said. "If the nest is completed by morning, maybe they'll not desert it if we move the box to the red oak."

"What's wrong with letting it sit here?" Henry asked. "Might be fun to watch them. At least they won't hit us every time we come out of the door as the barn swallows that built on the porch a few years back did."

The swallows had built when we were absent, and their babies had also been hatched when we were not there. So when we did come, the parents thought we were trespassing on their property and henceforth tried to stab us each time we left or entered the house! That was one family of children whose growing up we welcomed with relief. The wrens, much more friendly and much smaller, would give us no trouble.

Next morning, after sleeping until nine, we went out to investigate. The box was literally stuffed with heavy twigs. Not even a mouse could have built in it.

"Oh, it's one of their false nests!" I said. "You know, wren build false nests to prevent other wrens from coming into their territory! The little rascals!"

"I'll keep my eyes open," said Henry, "and find out where their real nest is."

"It's probably the one between your workshop and the granary. That pair is used to us, and since they were the first to build in the parking area, they think the whole place belongs to them."

One morning Henry said, "Ruth, have you noticed a wren going into the yard pump? I thought I saw one enter the pipe yesterday, and I'm sure I saw her do it today."

"What in the world would she want inside the pipe?" I asked.

Later that day Betty and Mike Fravel, Howard's niece and nephew, came over to see whether they might fish in our swimming pool.

"Yes, while I am at the house," I said, "but not after I leave. You know our rule about fishing there only when an adult is present."

"Yes, Mrs. Pochmann," said Mike.

"Can I have a drink at the pump?" asked Betty.

"Yes, dear. Use the dipper." I referred to the white enameled cup we had hung on the oak for thirsty fishermen who might come when we are not at home.

Mike grasped the handle and began to pump vigorously. Soon from out of the spout burst dirty water and twigs and bits of trash.

"Drat that wren!" I exclaimed and then explained to the children that the wrens considered the pump a good place for a nest and that, though they did not want it for themselves, they wanted to make sure no other wren would use it, so they had filled it with trash.

Our work in improving nesting areas and feeding places for birds probably brings us no net profit except a song on the wind, but the hope that we are helping these amazing little creatures is enough to keep us at it.


I have been asked whether I do most of my writing while at the farm. The answer is no. Ideas come as I watch the grace of a hawk or listen to the clear, insistent cry of a whippoorwill as he sings in the sandy barn road. But the whole, the entire poem, doesn't come until some time later, after I am in Madison with hours to myself. And that time comes in midwinter only, and then only if I plan ahead.

For example, I once tried to write something for August Derleth's poetry journal, *Hawk and Whippoorwill*. Fortified with pencil and paper, I walked up Psycho Path thinking of the bird we had whistled up to the farmhouse the night before. While resting on the screened porch, Henry and I had heard him in the poplar woods upstream. Henry, lying in the hammock, whistled loud and clear four times, imitating the three, sometimes four notes of the whippoorwill. There was a five-second silence. Henry whistled again. Then an answer came; the bird had moved much closer. Henry whistled twice; the bird sang twice. This "conversing" was repeated many times, the bird moving in until he was sitting above the driveway in one of our big willows.

Henry wearied of the sport. So I took up the call. Soon I had no task at all, for the bird didn't stop for an answer. He repeated his song dozens of times without pausing.

"Let's count," I whispered to Henry.

"Gosh, no!"

He sat up noiselessly, picked up his shoes, and walked in his sock feet to his bedroom. As he passed me, I whispered, "Don't turn on your light for a while."

"Haven't you had enough?"

The bird had waited, silent, while this movement was going on. But after Henry had closed the door to the living room, the song began again, and I counted. Two hundred and twenty-five times he sang "Whip-poor-will," then paused for three seconds and sang it three hundred and forty-five times more. He flew up the drive to the barn and continued to sing from his favorite rut in the sand. I gave up and went to bed.

In Derleth's *Walden West* he says he once counted fifteen hundred and seven consecutive calls in unbroken succession. He speaks of the whippoorwill as the "disembodied voice of the night itself, of the very earth brooding in the darkness," and to him, the sensitive man of nature that he is, the voice

awakens homesickness, intense longing. To me it is no more
a part of the country night than is the soft keening of the
owl or the clear little voice of the wood pewee or the loud
croaking of the bullfrogs on the pond bank, or even the
moonlight. Without the whippoorwill's cry, though, I am
sure I'd feel the night lacked something; I'd go to bed feeling I was turning in too soon.

Be that as it may, on this specific day I wanted to compare the voice of this bird with the voice of a poet. Up
Psycho Path I trudged, trying to keep my thoughts on the
problem, to liken a poet's voice to the whippoorwill's and
a poet's spirit to that of the soaring hawk.

Halfway up the hill I was distracted by a slight noise. To
my right was the ancient oak which, storm-torn and winter-
thrashed while still a juvenile, had grown into a distorted
thing, more horizontal than vertical, barely a tree at all
among its majestic neighbors, the pines. Bough after bough
had died and dropped off, creating deep litter on the ground,
which was mixed now with blown brown needles. Indeed,
only one leafy branch rose from the eighteen-inch trunk.
But it was not the living part of the tree at which I looked.
It was the life within the tree: a baby raccoon. His mirth-
provoking face peered at me from a big hole in the trunk:
triangular face, dark eyes above the black mask, small round
ears. Should I continue on my way or step over to see what
I could see? I stepped over, the face was swallowed by the
darkness of the den, and I saw nothing. I had a strong urge
to poke with a stick, but if my probing should frighten away
this interesting family, I would be the greater loser. So I
quietly resumed my climb.

Once on top of Big Ridge and settled into the long blue-
grass under Lone Oak, with pad on my knee and pencil in
hand, I gazed into the sky, awaiting inspiration. A pigeon

hawk sailed over Fenskes' bean field, but nearer, a rough-legged hawk glided downward over our stream.

I wrote:

> A hawk on the wing is a lovesome thing,
> His soaring and gliding define pure grace.

The bird had disappeared. The thought occurred to me that he had seen one of our young pheasants and had swooped on him. The next two lines were:

> A hawk on the ground is a loathesome thing,
> Clutching, devouring, and shrewd of face.

Now that would never do if I were to liken a poet's spirit to that of a hawk. I tried again:

> The spirit of a poet must rise and swing
> Like hawk aloft, the sky to pace—
> His not the cry of the hawk on the wing
> But that of the bird with the homely face.

Not good. I drew a line through it, then I sat for a while. The smells were wonderful that morning. The black-cherry tree a few feet away enticed me. I had never seen it so full, and the cherries must be at the peak of ripeness, for some had already fallen, and their peculiar fragrance took my mind from birds and poets. Stubbornly, though, I dragged my thoughts back to the subject and wrote:

> The flight of a hawk
> is the shape of a poet's dream.
> The song of a bird
> is the soul's outcry.
>
> Shifting sand in the dim roadway
> where wheel has furrowed
> and hoof has pressed—

No more words would come. I sat and sat. The cherry fragrance grew more pungent. They are very fat this year, I thought, and would be delicious with a little sugar and a scoop of ice cream, or made into cherry butter or jelly.

With that I quickly fashioned four cups of the paper from the pad and joyfully filled them, propping each full cup in the grass until the others were ready. Then carefully, two cups in each hand, I descended by way of the south slope, which is more gentle and smooth.

And that's the way it always is when I try to write at Triple Ridge. Too much, too near.

By November the departure of all flowers and most of the songbirds leaves us strangely lonely. It is then I most appreciate the Pine Room. I take a book and a sandwich or, more often, a writing pad and Coke and walk up the farm road by the barn to where the beach heather grows, then turn into the pines at the weathered stump. Almost at once I am in the room.

Long ago, when the basement of the farmhouse was finished, some leftover rocks and boulders were dumped on the hillside, and later pines were planted around them. Deer were able to travel through the maze of lower branches; indeed, they could do so without disturbing the snow that lay thick along each limb. But man could not penetrate them. So I took my little saw one day and cut off all the dead limbs and all the lower branches to the height of my head—all, that is, in a circle around the rocks—leaving the outside row of trees untouched, for those branches were still fresh and full of green needles.

The "room" I made is about twenty feet in diameter, and the beautiful gray and brown rocks, partially covered with pale-green lichen, are clustered in the center. It's a restful, sequestered place, from which one can see out but cannot be seen. The carpet is of resilient pine needles, most fragrant in November, for this is the time when pines shed their old needles.

The inner wall of the Pine Room toward the top of the hill is still impenetrable to man, except for one exit I made with my little saw. I extended that exit into a path four feet wide, running crookedly through the thick-growing jack pines to a gnarled oak, then up to the abandoned fox holes, past the black oak that has split in two, and on up and up and up to the top of Big Ridge, where blow the *Viola pedata* and the coral bells. This is Psycho Path. I defy anyone to climb this route and take his troubles with him! Pine Room is a good place in which to check them.

I have a wee friend in Pine Room—Dartmouth, a chipmunk that lives beneath one of the rocks. Dartmouth's doorway is clean and smooth, but tucked under the edge of the rock may be a corncob he has hauled all the way from a bird feeder; he nibbles on the golden kernels from his secure space, watching me but not afraid. I talk to him and, with slow motion, pitch him a crumb or two of bread; if it falls near him, he will come out and pick it up in his cunning front feet, tremble his whiskers at me, and eat it on the spot. After snow blankets the rocks, his burrow's entrance is completely hidden, and he goes into his long winter sleep.

Both hill and pines hold back the wind and bend it toward the barn. Hence in April, the month of wind and windflower, I go often to Pine Room in search of calm. Dartmouth then is the busiest creature. One would think, from the frequency of his trips out and in, that he has the seasons mixed and is now storing for the winter. With his pouches puffed out he comes home and, with scarcely a glance at me, runs into his cavity beneath the stone and deposits his load of seeds; in a minute or two his perky face appears, and this time he looks me squarely in the eye. I speak to him and he emerges daintily and quickly to sit up and "chip" at me. Sometimes he brings another chipmunk home; she is his choice for the season, and together they raise their young beneath the cool rock. I cannot tell the wife from the husband, for they are equally bright rusty brown on their black-and-beige striped backs, tawny brown on their cheeks, and almost red on their flanks. By species they are the Eastern chipmunk.

On a few of my visits to Pine Room I write a little, but most of the time I am too busy observing. Since I am hidden, I can watch birds taking a sand bath among the patches of beach heather outside. And in the winter I can often see the pine siskin as it clings on a cone to eat the pine seeds. In summer I have found a few small nests far out on the ends of pine branches about fifteen feet above ground, which I surmise are nests of the siskin, though as yet I have not actually seen him building or using the nests.

His companions in flight are usually goldfinch, crossbills, and redpolls. The crossbills place their nests in similar locations, but ornithologists have told me that few crossbills nest this far west. Goldfinch nests are a different shape, nice little cups, and are most often in meadow shrubs five or six feet from the ground. Nests of redpolls, if found this far south at all, are usually in willows and paper birches. So my conclusion, unofficially, is that those around the Pine Room and along Psycho Path belong to the siskins. They are easy birds to identify because they are brown-streaked all over and not more than five inches long; their bills are rather more slender than those of seed-eating birds like sparrows, for, though siskins eat seeds in winter, they eat insects in summer. When they fly, they show yellow in wings and tail.

It has been said that there is always music in a woods if one has ears to hear it. Well, I can hear more on some days than on others, and in the Pine Room I listen better. The music of the pines is quite different from that of the oaks. In the Wildwood, where oaks are predominant, I hear the soft rubbing of the rough branches and the ecstatic kissing of their leaves; but the wind in the tops of the pines makes a light clicking music, with an occasional off-key squeak that makes me smile. The pine music is like a junior-high band, the oak like a symphony orchestra, and the wind is the hum that ties the instruments together.

# VIII  *Henry and the Trout Stream*

A N Y T H I N G that stirs and delights a man and at the
same time fills his heart with peace is a good thing. For
Henry this is primarily the stream, though its improvement
has meant work that was often grueling for a professor of
literature.

During the years prior to our acquisition of the farm
Henry spent many hours on streams studying the ways of
trout, their cover and food, their spawning grounds, their
selection of pools, and the temperature of the water, so that

when he acquired a mile of stream of his own, he was ready to begin working out some of his theories.

His biggest handicap was the lack of another man to help him handle stones and logs. That was his primary reason for buying a tractor. By experimenting, he learned how to make it and its accessories work efficiently for him. He wrestled logs down the steep hillsides without ruining the patches of huckleberry and young maples. After Howard Fravel's warning and instruction Henry learned to drag logs to within six feet of the stream bank and then roll them into the water by foot and cant hook, sort of nudging them in so they wouldn't cause a landslide.

He figured out how to tie in logs diagonally so water would wash out a deep run and make a feeding pool below as it flowed over or around the log; this must be done in a way to hasten rather than slow down the current. At first he used wire to tie the logs against driven posts, but the posts themselves washed out when water rushed beneath the log. So he later tied together with strong wire two heavy rocks and saddled them over the log. This weight was enough, ordinarily, to keep them in place during flood stage, but sometimes, despite his care, a few turned loose and traveled around a bend or two in the stream bed. He was able to utilize them, however, where they came to rest by tying them under the banks to help hold up the loose sand until his plantings could take hold.

Four years after he began his log work, he checked to see which logs had been successful in making pools that trout will use. He found that the logs against or almost against the banks had been 90 per cent successful. Those laid across the current had been 100 per cent *un*successful. Those laid out in the middle, straight with the current, had been only moderately successful. Those laid diagonally, with the upper end against the bank and the lower end downstream several feet from the bank, were the best. These last were the wing dams and they were, fortunately, the most numerous. Except for those logs that have been displaced by floods following the Big Thaw, nearly all the others have since been made into wing dams.

Another Henry-built structure for improvement is the log revetment. At first, in several long stretches, the steep banks were entirely bare where sloughing off had occurred during floods and freshets. These eroded banks were depositing silt, which covered the gravel in the stream bed and thereby discouraged trout ready to spawn. Our first Conservation Department shrubs went into those banks and soon sent down their deep roots and spread their shallow ones to hold the sandy soil in place. Along the base of these eroded places Henry built revetments.

First he drove oak posts into the stream bed, in a row parallel with the bank. They were about five or six feet high above ground and about four feet apart. Behind them he laid small logs, big logs, large branches, and clumps of dense prairie grass. This grass often took root; even when it didn't, it served to catch and hold seeds that blew into the logs until they could germinate and put forth their own tenacious roots. The digging and packing of the sod took a long time. I seldom helped, but Eddie Wentland's son Bob worked with Henry when Howard Fravel was working for Phil Sawin or the bowling alley manager at Pleasant Lake.

"I can build only one revetment in a weekend," sighed Henry, "and then only if I've already hauled the logs to the bank. Otherwise I have to allow two weekends."

"But your payoff is good," I reminded him. "It's satisfying to know you're using good management and saving something valuable. It's gratifying, too, to see the revetments furnishing new homes for all the little marsh birds. I saw a long-billed marsh wren and a song sparrow in one today, and a chipmunk too."

Of great help to him in his planning was an illustrated pamphlet from the watershed-management section of the Wisconsin Conservation Department. This contains detailed drawings of log, rock, and sod revetments, of various deflector constructions, "digger" logs, and tree "rip-rap cover" to control erosion and silt deposit on sharp bends. This is free material and so explicit that amateurs like us can follow the instructions. The Fenskes used this pamphlet when making a concrete V-deflector to create a nice fifty-by-one-hundred-foot pool on their part of the Wedde just beyond our fence. The Public Service Commission permits this open-center deflector, for it allows the usual amount of water to flow out, whereas a dam would not.

"I'm going to walk the stream," said Henry one day after a heavy rain. He pulled on his rubber boots, slid into his slicker, and put on his red visored cap.

"May I go too? Walking just after a rain is great fun."

"Your boots leak."

"I know. I'm not going into the water. I just want to prune some branches where they are growing too thick and too high. First thing we know they will shade the water so much that no cress will grow."

We walked together down the bridge road, but at the bridge we parted; he stepped through the willows into the water and I took the high path on the north side of the stream. I knew what he would do. Since the rain had washed plenty of food from the fields into the stream, he would not waste time trying to fish, but he would check the banks for new fissures, and when he found one he'd do something to forestall the loss of great hunks of soil. He would observe flood currents. He would see where he could slow down the runoff from the watershed so the ground might absorb more moisture, recharging the underground supplies that eventually enter the stream through springs, slowly, assuring a good supply in dry seasons as well as wet. Walking the stream was, therefore, as fruitful in its way as his fishing it usually was. And he seemed to enjoy it as much.

I went along the path, checking and admiring the crab apples and grape vines, which by then were in their fourth year and were forming a thicket that held a dozen or more bird nests. I recalled my feeling of dismay when first I saw how close together they had been planted by Damaske and Jones, but now I could see why. The vines were clinging and curling around the branches, which were so interlaced that it was difficult to see which belonged to which trunk. The resultant thicket made for small birds a fine shelter from hawks and owls. And as both trees and vines produced fruit the thicket was an excellent wildlife attraction.

When opposite the point where the paper birches were growing too thick, I returned to the streamside to prune them. Several trout, like quick shadows, darted beneath the cress growing around Henry's logs. The cress and the overhanging grasses were the trout's protection and feeding ground. I was tempted to gather some cress for dinner. It had not yet begun to bloom and would be very tender as well as delightfully spicy. But the pruning really needed to be done, and my time was short. So I delved into the job.

I like to prune. I size up the tree or shrub and picture it as I want it to be. Then I consider the surrounding plants, the effect on them of my pruning the tree. Sometimes then my first plan is changed. In this case I wanted to thin the trees so the selected ones could grow larger and faster; I wanted to allow sunlight to reach the watercress, and I wanted to make a prettier picture, allowing more of the black-and-white trunks to show.

Henry came around the curve. "Making progress?" he wanted to know.

"Not yet. Just making decisions."

"Don't cut them all down. We want them to keep the water cool enough for brooks. Remember that they need colder water than rainbows do."

The water was cold enough, both Virginia and I knew, for we had often tried to wade on the hottest days of July and August. After a few minutes we had stepped out with blue feet. Ray White told us the temperature of our stream was consistently at 58°. The Wisconsin *Conservation Bulletin* says brook trout need temperatures of from 60° to 70°, while brown and rainbows can stand up to 75°. But for the hatching of the eggs the temperature must be colder. Since brook and brown trout spawn in the fall and winter (the rainbows in early spring), their eggs are sure to be in colder water.

On the way back to the house that day I stopped at a bank where willows had grown so close together they formed another thicket. During our first spring, in our eagerness to plant every spot that had been denuded by grazing, we had stuck in about a hundred willow branches cut from our one weeping willow in Madison (cut after the sap had begun to rise but before the buds had begun to swell). All had taken root in the moist sand and were now threatening one another. I had been eager to thin them. Now was my chance. I cut them off at the ground, leaving only six! Hastily drag-

ging the tops behind a clump of red osier dogwood, I hoped
I was hiding them from Henry, who was proud of the way
they had sprouted.

"He'll see them, though, if he returns along this path.
He's got six eyes!" I said to myself.

When he came in for dinner, the first thing he said was,
"Why did you cut the willows?"

"Same reason I cut the birches; too many, too thick. They
were strangling one another. I left six, you know. Some of
those will eventually have to be cut too." I was on the de-
fensive.

"I'm glad you cut them. If you hadn't, I would have. We
made a mistake in putting so many there. They are on the
wrong side of the stream too. Since I fish dry fly, my back-
casts are apt to catch on branches on the north bank. The
tall-growing things on the south bank aren't nearly so trou-
blesome, except on bends."

Trout have increased remarkably as a result of his constant
awareness of their requirements. He thinks the Wedde now
contains as many as it can support.

"It is, after all, only a small stream. There just isn't enough
water for hundreds of fish. Fortunately only four of us give
it a workout regularly. It couldn't stand the sort of fishing
given to the Mecan or even to the smaller Chaffee."

Bob Pooley asked Henry whether our stream were stocked
with hatchery fish. Bob was another professor-guest.

"No. And that's the way I like it," said Henry. "Hatchery
fish are easier to catch, but I prefer to fish for native fish,
which provide better sport. They're wilier—hard to raise and
full of tricks after you've hooked them."

"He ties his own flies, too, Bob," I said. "To fish for na-
tives with flies he himself has tied has a flavor of the primi-

tive. Without that, fishing as a sport would lose some of its allure. Agree?"

Henry smiled. "Most fishermen don't feel like that. The streams that have been stocked with Conservation fish catch hell on opening day and all season, in fact. Since the planted fish are easier to fool with lures and man-made flies, the Mecan, the White, and the Chaffee bear the crowds. I don't mind falling over logs, but I don't enjoy stumbling over fishermen. I like leisurely fishing."

Our stream is posted, though the signs say that permission will be given if requested at the house. In Wisconsin "No Trespassing" signs mean that a man must stay in the water while he fishes; if he sets foot on the bank, he is trespassing unless he has permission from the owner of the land. Friends who now fish the Wedde understand what Henry has tried to do; they don't trample our plantings, break down the revetments, leave tin cans in the water, or throw burning cigarettes in the dry grass.

Henry enjoys fishing even when his creel is empty, but it is so seldom without fish that I questioned him at length.

"Why are you more successful than your friends?"

"I think it's because I don't concentrate on just the open water but fish every little nook and corner. Other fishermen think that's unproductive water, or they pass it up as too hard to cover with a dry fly."

I have noticed other stratagems too. He is careful when in the water not to make unnecessary vibrations such as are caused when a man bumps against a log. He wades carefully so as not to send waves ahead to advertise his approach. If he accidentally or clumsily puts fish down, he often waits a few minutes to let things return to normal before sending out an exploratory fly. He thinks talking does not disturb trout but that light colors do. Accordingly he wears neutral gray and beige or brown, never white, for trout can see well and are easily put down by reflections.

He uses light-weight tackle because it is sportier and more easily, more deftly handled than heavy.

He always fishes dry fly, the kind that is fished upstream and floated on the surface of the water. Some of his friends prefer a wet fly, which is fished downstream and below the surface. The wet-fly angler's line is seldom out of the water and can be threaded through overhanging brush.

"But mine is constantly whipped back and forth," he said, to Bob Pooley, "so I need more open water. I can usually shoot my fly through a narrow channel ahead of me, but if I don't have a fairly open lane for my back-cast, I'm in constant trouble.

"Sometimes," he continued, "I resort to roll-casting or bow-casting. Both methods are effective, but I'm getting too old to last long at that sort of fishing. Too tiring."

"Show Bob the Pochmann Hopper," I suggested. Then to Bob I said, "He's prouder of that fly than of any book he's ever written."

"It's probably given more pleasure," said Henry.

He modestly took the fly from his box and handed it to Bob.

"His friend, the late Chubby Goodlad," I said, "liked this fly so much when Henry made one for him that he showed it to a professional tier, who later made it and named it for Henry. It is now made commercially by the Weber Fly-Tying Co. of Stevens Point."

"Do you use it all season or just when grasshoppers come to your area?" Bob wanted to know.

"When the hoppers come. Before that time I use chiefly the Gray Hackle with a peacock body and the Royal Coachman with polar-bear wings. I tie them both sparsely. And during the mayfly season I use my big white and yellow fly, tied spent-wing. That's a pattern very hard to tie just right. For one thing, it's a big fly, so unless it's tied sparsely it hits the water too hard. It must drop as light as a feather, just as a mayfly does."

The mayfly hatch along the trout streams is a pleasant event for trout fishermen, not at all like the enormous hatches over the Mississippi River at La Crosse, where the big bridge has to be closed during the hours when these delicate gauze-like insects make their mating flights. They cover automobiles, blanketing windshields and lights; they swarm around streetlights too. But along the streams there are no lights to pull the insects into great concentrations. Therefore relatively few emerge at a time, just enough to set trout wildly feeding.

Edwin W. Teale says the mayfly lives for two years in the mud or sand of the stream bed, molting many times, and that only in its final molting is it airborne.

"Then, after mating, it dies," said Henry. "Its whole life span outside water is only a few minutes."

Though the insect is called the mayfly, it doesn't really hatch in central Wisconsin until early June. At that time Henry wants to fish the Mecan River from just after sunset until about ten o'clock, for that is when the hatch takes place. The Mecan, larger than other streams in the immediate area, has more mayflies. Trout measuring twenty-two to twenty-four inches are not unusual catches on the Mecan during the hatch.

While Henry was building a rustic footbridge across the stream two bends down from the tractor bridge, I did a little landscaping there with some native plants, forget-me-nots and shinleaf, that I found on the new acreage we bought

from Phil Sawin—twenty acres adjoining and west of our
original purchase. The succulent leaves of shinleaf, a *Pyrola*,
were once used as plasters for wounds, but I used this low
rich green plant as a ground cover under dogwood. The
forget-me-nots became a blue carpet in June along the curv-
ing banks. They thrive in either deep shade or partial sun
but bloom far better with some sunlight.

Henry spent a good deal of his time in 1965 on the dam
near the guest cottage. Each big rain caused a problem. He
and Howard Fenske worked at it together for a day, but
then Howard was called to Wautoma to work with the
Conservation Department's fire-fighting unit. Henry continued alone, hauling rocks and oak boards and making a
frame. He packed in sod and soil. It was backbreaking, but
he was gratified to count eighteen trout in the pool the day
after he finished. Some were small, one was big. The big one
fed with just a soft "sup" sound, but the little ones made
big splashes.

He fished for an hour downstream by the rustic bridge
and caught six, plate-size.

"That was fun," he reported when he came in for dinner.
"I must have raised thirty little fellows—six inches. Threw
'em all back. Should make them more wary next time I
float a fly over them."

Though six inches is the legal limit, Henry rarely keeps a
trout under eight inches unless it is hurt. He cleans his trout
as he catches them; then when he brings them to the kitchen,
there is nothing to do except scrape them a little. Trout have
few scales. He rinses them under running water and lays
them on paper towels to dry. I lay them on a platter and
cover them with foil to refrigerate or to freeze. Since freezing dries them out rather quickly, I try to use them early.
Sometimes I cook and bone them before freezing, and I then
use the shredded fish in casseroles.

We prefer trout broiled, with butter and salt, or fried in hot fat after being rolled in corn meal and salt. I rarely serve a highly seasoned sauce with trout; the natural flavor of the fish is so delicious that we think sauce is superfluous.

The late Professor Bill Hesseltine was vastly amused by my implicit faith in Henry's ability to catch fish. I once invited two dozen people to have a trout dinner with us on a Sunday evening. Bill declared that I invited them while my husband was out fishing on the preceding Friday afternoon. Since stream trout cannot be bought, Bill thought I was taking a big chance. What he didn't know was that I had twenty-four trout in my freezer. Henry brought home his limit anyway, so our guests had seconds.

For Henry his work on the stream is play. It relaxes while exercising him. He doesn't push himself at stream jobs, as he has a tendency to do in other areas. If he sees a woodchuck sunning on a log, he stops to observe the color and condition of his fur, his size, and the nearness of the animal to his hole. If he sees a flower that he thinks I am not familiar with, he remembers where it is so I can find it. If a branch has fallen into the water, he gets out his pocketknife to smooth the torn trunk of the parent shrub or tree. He sometimes sits in a worn canvas chair near the bridge to rest, to watch, and to contemplate. From that vantage point he has a limited panoramic view of a stretch of stream, all of Birch Pond, some of the birch and maple woodland, the hillside, the fen meadow, the waterfall, a marsh filled with poison hemlock (Socrates' hemlock) and Norway spruce, and a thicket of wild crab apple and virgin's-bower (wild clematis). He says he is king of all he surveys.

Izaak Walton had five rules for himself. One of them was to take pleasure while you are working toward your goal, have enjoyment along the way. Both of us live by that rule, particularly when working on or near the stream, for it has that kind of beauty that extends the imagination. One would have to be verily stupid not to expand inwardly at sight of the perennial color on the banks. Perhaps the most voluptuous season is late summer. It is then that jewelweed drips its apricot lanterns above the watercress, and goldenrod stands up to meet the bee-covered purple asters and swamp milkweed; bright blue "bottles" of closed gentian compete with their own reflection; the meadow furnishes a backdrop of lavender bergamot and dusty-pink joe-pye weed. It is then that wild cucumber twines its long tresses over ninebark and cranberry, thrusting ivory spires upward like many small candles, and clematis, trying to follow, stops short and spreads its feathery seed clusters, like a bridal veil, over sedges.

Isaac Walton would have approved our sharing with friends both our pleasure and our work. Another of his rules was that one should be grateful for opportunity and attainment and be ready to share them, for, he said, little would any of us have if our luck were not better than we deserved.

His third and fourth rules were to seek what you want by fair means so that you will have no bitterness toward men, and to spend little time on that which angers or vexes you but much time on that which brings quietness and confidence and cheer. We're working on that one, for it seems logical to think that all creative action is based on confidence and on faith: confidence in what one wants to accomplish, and faith in one's ability to do it.

His fifth rule is one which we feel would be a tough one for us: desire nothing so much that you will be unhappy without it. If we were to lose this farm, or if the stream were to go dry, it would take a lot of trying for us to create something else to take its place.

Up until last year we had bank swallows. They built their

horizontal burrows, two or three feet deep, at the top of the only bare steep bank on our section of the stream. At the far end of the burrow was the nest, made of soft grasses. (I must confess that I dug into one to find out how it was made.) Henry had to ruin the "community" early last spring when he discovered that during the winter erosion had taken place, dislodging a big chunk of the bank, which then slid into the stream and ruined a deep hole he had made for trout; also the slide exposed roots of some nice pines growing at the top of the bank.

"Ruth, will you help me dig turf from the pool bank? I'll pack it solid on the front of that bare place. It will close the swallows' nests, but that can't be helped. I must stop the erosion."

"Wait till I put on my boots and get my shovel."

We worked for an hour before I grew tired and returned to the house. He continued for another two hours and was exhausted when he came in.

"Too weary to eat dinner?" I asked.

"Yes, afraid so," he sighed, making for the bathroom to wash his muddy hands and face.

"Want to rest first?"

He slept for two hours. I was reading in the kitchen when he came in at eight o'clock.

"I could have slept straight on till eight tomorrow morning," he declared. "I want only a glass of milk."

I had learned from previous similar situations not to insist that he eat when he was overtired. So we both went to bed for the night.

After I had turned off my light, I lay thinking about those swallows, how pretty they looked skimming the pond for insects, how distinctive was the elongated white "heart" on the breast below the dark collar. We mustn't forget, I thought, to visit the Fenskes' farm during the barn swallows' nesting time, when hundreds come to that barn and plaster the entire east wall with truncated cones of mud bonded with grass.

Suddenly I heard a weird crying outside. Skipper barked once and then was quiet. I stepped to the south window and listened. Toward the near brush pile the sound came again. It was a kind of rasping bark. Was it a raccoon? Was he in pain? Was he crying for a mate? Or was he vaguely discontented with his lot and finding solace in the sound of his moaning?

The chill night air sent a shiver through me and I let the window down, but I stood for a minute admiring the pines in the starlight. Then I returned to bed.

Pulling the star-patterned quilt up to my chin, I worried a little more about our swallows. Where would they go now? The nearest steep banks I could think of were in the gravel pit at Coloma, but no water was there. Maybe they would build along the Mecan River at the picnic grounds known as The Pines. The mossy banks there were steep on one side of the river, though marshy on the other. My last conscious thought was that I'd miss the swallows' twittering and chattering and shimmering grace . . .

Ray White grew into a man, and his boyhood interest in wildlife became his profession. Specializing in fish, he worked with the Conservation Department for several years after obtaining his degree at the University, and he is still a visitor at Triple Ridge, though often now as a researcher. For two years he came with groups of men to shock our trout for scientific purposes.

Shocking is an interesting undertaking to watch. One man wearing a harness walks up the stream center pulling a canvas float on which are a storage battery, a large zinc tub, an improvised desk with writing pad and pencil, and a measuring stick. On each side and ahead of the float is a man with an electrode. He pushes the electrode into all portions of the stream likely to harbor fish. As the stunned fish come to the surface, a fourth man picks them up in a long-handled net and drops them into the tub. A fifth man takes the measurement of the fish, makes his notation on the pad, and examines the fins to determine whether there is a clipped place; a clipped fin will tell him that this fish has stayed around since the last shocking. By this time the fish shows signs of consciousness and is returned to the stream.

When the men have finished checking the fish, they determine water flow, the number of gallons per minute. All this information is of value to the Department and to the professors at the University who are engaged in such research.

We at Triple Ridge have long kept records of one kind or another, hoping they will be of use to professionals. I record the length of time Henry fishes our stream, the date, the number and size of fish he catches, and the kind, whether brook or German brown. Such a record for ten successive years may tell something to professional researchers. I also record in my daily journal the dates of (1) the first wild flower of each variety, (2) my harvest of wild fruit, (3) the first killing frost in autumn. This record will eventually go to Professor James Zimmerman, who is compiling such data for the entire state.

Virginia's experiments and records made during her high-school days and first two years of University work pertained chiefly to the pool. She recorded clearness and temperature of the water, approximate number of fish, their spawning success, and survival after the winter freeze-over; she listed and described their predators and tried to determine whether most winterkill was due to predators or to lack of oxygen and food under the ice. She fed live fresh-water shrimp and *Daphnia* to her aquarium fish, noting effects. With her father she examined the water plants in the ponds and stream—water buttercup, chara, cress, grass, sedges—and noted the kinds of life other than fish that lived in them: aquatic worms, encased caddisworms, mayfly larvae, snails, fresh-water shrimp, clams.

Henry has made few records, but he is constantly experimenting, and when he comes to conclusions, he promptly tells a professional about his activity. For instance, when he discovered which of the log structures was most effective and which the most useless, he told Ray and his cohorts. When he and the Fenskes built three different types of open-center dams, he showed them to Ray and stood by while the pools behind them were checked for fish and plant life.

One day Virginia was looking for fresh-water clams in the Wedde, like those she had found as a child in the Mecan. Crayfish, too, she wanted to find, but neither seemed to be in this smaller stream. She did find a gray stone, five by six inches, with two round holes and a third one that looked as if it had been begun but not finished. She pondered deeply about it. Neither Henry nor I knew what it was. The holes were smooth and about an inch deep. The first two were three inches apart, the third one only an inch from the second and about a quarter-inch deep. The bottom of the stone was almost flat, with short light scratches covering the center.

That afternoon she and I rode to Mr. Emil Schultz to ask about it.

"He's one of the oldest people around here," Virginia said. "He'll know."

When we got out of our car, she exclaimed, "Look! He has five stones like mine."

He did indeed. Five gray stones having smooth round holes lay beneath a bridal wreath near the Schultzes' back door.

Mr. Schultz smiled broadly as he took Virginia's stone from her.

"Ya," he said, his bright blue eyes a-twinkle, "we grow big earthworms at Richford."

"Ach!" said Virginia. "Don't you know, really?"

He turned the stone over and stuck his forefinger into each hole in turn.

"I've heard tell dat a Indian squaw drilled a hole in a stone every time she had a grandchild, just like today de women wear beads for dey grandchillen."

That was all she could get from him, but we came to a conclusion for ourselves and later had it confirmed by an archaeologist. It was an Indian hammer. The thumb fit into the first and largest hole, the forefinger into the second, and the shallow hole was a rest for the middle finger. The light scratches on the bottom were marks made during the hammering. It was not the usual Indian hammer head meant to be fastened on the end of a handle. (Henry insists the holey stones are remnants of bowling balls that got busted!)

All of Mr. Schultz's stones, as well as Virginia's, were found in the flowing streams. We haven't yet figured out why.

One day as I was sitting on the stream bank, Henry came up and said, "What you doing?"

"Cogitatin'."

"About what?"

"Possible effects the Russian satellite will have on civilization."

"Great Scot!"

That was while the first satellite was winging its historic flight around the earth.

"We might go up on Big Ridge tonight and watch for it," he said.

Shortly before the time forecast for its appearance near the western horizon, we put on our lightweight jackets against the cool night air and walked up to the top of the hill. Moonlight sifted through the pine needles to lace the ground with shadows and to silver the grass where we sat.

For a while we were silent, as we often are when outdoors at night. The great beautiful world around us was overwhelming, vast and full of mystery. Listening intently, I heard the music of tiny wings and remote murmurings, of leaves caressing their mothering branches, of crickets' cheer, and of a tinkling sound like sleigh bells. That was water bubbling in its own pools around the boulders and water wheel left stacked in the stream by the Wentland boys forty-five years ago.

The story was that both boys were deeply interested in electricity, but their father said it was just a newfangled expensive idea he couldn't afford; kerosene lanterns were good enough for him. The boys built a water-powered turbine in the stream, piling big rocks across the current and fixing a water wheel to trigger a small generator. Soon they had a string of dim electric lights up and down the creek, but Mr. John continued doing his barn chores by the light of his lantern.

"The moon is going to make it hard to see the satellite." Henry brought me back to the moment.

"It's still behind us," I said. "Maybe, though, we should be sitting in the shade of a tree."

"It's nice here. We can shade our eyes when the time comes."

So we sat on there in the open, with the whole western sky above us. Because of the moonlight, the only stars we could see plainly were in the west. Some were very bright, and whenever I concentrated on one, it twinkled excessively so that I wondered whether it might be the satellite.

"How fast does it travel?" I wanted to know. "Will it shoot across like a shooting star? Or will it travel more like an airplane light?"

"I guess like a plane."

Silence.

I wished for Virginia to share this experience with us. But she had moved that week into Barnard Hall on the University campus; her weekends with us in the future would be few. A sudden loneliness swept over me, and tears blurred the stars. I reached out for Henry's hand.

"I miss Virginia."

He crushed his cigarette in the sand and put his arm around my shoulders. Neither of us saw the satellite that night.

After a while we walked down the hill by way of the barn road, making almost no noise as our footsteps fell in sand.

"Maybe we'll see a fox or a deer," Henry said in a low voice.

Instead we were startled by a loud, clear "Whip-poor-will!" shouted from almost beneath our feet. The bird, as frightened by my "E-e-eek!" as I was, scurried into the pines, accompanied by Henry's laughter.

# IX "One Sees What One Knows"

W I T H Wherry's *Wild Flower Guide* in my jeans pocket,
I gathered specimens every time I went for a walk, every
Saturday and Sunday for four years. Then on Mondays I
took them to Professor Hugh Iltis, director of the herbarium
at the University of Wisconsin in Madison. He told me that
very little research had been done in Waushara County and
that he'd be grateful for my help.

"Amateurs can help professionals a lot," he said. "We get
out for occasional short trips, but you are there frequently

on one specific site and can keep up with the seasons week after week. You say you've had no training in botany. No matter. You can help tremendously anyway by bringing me specimens. Tell you what I'll do." He hurried over to his desk and brought me a thin white card on which were printed a map of Wisconsin, a map of a specific county, and the words "Township," "Section," and "Range." Spaces were left for the finder of a plant to write in the kind of place, that is, the kind of soil, moisture, and shade in which the plant was found. Even the accompanying plants were to be noted if known.

"I'll print your name here," he said, "and the numbers of town, section, and range so you won't have to write them in every time. You fill in the data about the plant and give the date." He picked up a stack of newspapers bound tightly together with boards on top and bottom. "These are press boards," he explained. "This is one way to preserve your specimens. You may take along such boards today."

A week later I received several hundred little cards with the promised printing on them and a map of Waushara County. With a red pencil I made a dot to show the location of Triple Ridge Farm. Each week I spent hours pressing the flowers so they would dry properly, without mildewing, and so that each stem, the petals, and both sides of the leaves could be seen for study. As the number of varieties grew to three hundred, my excitement over each new one increased. Henry brought me a clump of dainty cress he had found on the stream bank; Virginia brought me a tiny sunbright blossom from the Dump. I was often coming upon small orchids in the wettest part of the meadow and shadiest part of the hillsides. My exhilaration was comparable to that of a collector of Tiffany glass who comes upon a rare piece at an auction and gets it for a few dollars.

Friends who went with us often got into the spirit of the search. Miss Ruth Wallerstein, late scholar on the University faculty, had a quick eye for the smallest flowers and found some I had not seen, including brook lobelia and spiraling lady's-tresses. Miss Helen White, late novelist, professor, and at that time national president of the American Association of University Women and a member of UNESCO, found for me the first lovely yellow blossom of the obnoxious weed known as goatsbeard. Together she and I examined its flat, many-petaled flower, which has prominent pointed green sepals between the petals.

Each season new seeds blow in and spring into flowers I am not familiar with, or produce old friends I've known since my childhood in East Texas. I recall the warm feeling in my heart the day I found a spring beauty at the edge of the Wildwood. Spring beauties in Texas peep from under lush clover and color the lawns a delicate pink; we used to pull handfuls of them to decorate our bonnets and to stuff into our apron pockets, but at Triple Ridge I treasure every single flower, for it does not grow in abundance.

Now, in 1968, my list of flora is roughly divided so: more than seven hundred varieties of flowers, more than two hundred trees and shrubs, but only a few ferns and mosses and grasses, and even fewer sedges and lichens, for I have not yet learned to recognize differences in their varieties. Mushrooms and fungi are another field still ahead for me to study and enjoy; few are included in my list.

When Emerson wrote, "That day is good on which we have the most perceptions," he must have been out for a walk in May. That is the month for arrival of most of the warblers in Wisconsin. Rhubarb spears are red and tender, and the hills are blue with bird's-foot violets.

No one knowledgeable in the ways of nature can cover

much ground in May. There are too many wonders underfoot and overhead.

Pasqueflowers and wild buttercups have earlier ushered in the season. The pasque has blown away its purple beauty by May Day (white or light lavender when it opens, it later turns to orchid, to rose, to purple), but the waxy buttercup lingers to greet the violets: the fragrant miniature *viola blanda* on the stream bank, the big blue swamp violet on the hummocks of sphagnum moss in the bogs, the large white Canada and the downy yellow violets in the Wildwood, and the fast-spreading Confederate on the bank of the pool. Several other kinds of violets are there, but the most spectacular is the bird's-foot, *Viola pedata*, so called because the deeply serrated leaf resembles the shape of a bird's foot. I once counted twenty blossoms on one plant, each bloom the size of a quarter. No leaves showed above the blossoms. Great mats of these lovely plants grow in the sand, and their blooming periods depend on the amount of sun they get; altogether, their season at Triple Ridge extends over six weeks.

The Wildwood floor is deep with forest litter, and coming through it, fresh and fragile, are hundreds of big *Trillium grandiflorum*, its three leaves wide and succulent and its three petals snow-white. This flower I introduced from oak woods a few miles south of us. By the time the smaller native nodding trillium blooms in our moist bog gardens, the larger trillium has turned shell-pink.

Across the drive among the oaks are May apples, mandrakes, their hidden waxy white blossoms as lovely as any flowers I know. In the moist spots grow dogtooth violets, better named trout lilies.

Lilies of the valley carpet the ground beneath the old-fashioned lilac, so thickly that I have to dig up some each spring to keep a path open from the porch to the asparagus bed at the foot of the hill. Now in May the air is delicious with their fragrance. Mrs. Wentland planted these lilies in 1914, but during our ownership they have multiplied a thousandfold because Henry removed a willow that had shaded them too much. They will grow in dense shade but will blossom better in partial sun.

Wind anemone whitens the swamp hummocks, and red trumpets of climbing honeysuckle further glorify chokecherry branches already dripping their perfect clusters, like white fringe, from every limb.

"Mother," said Virginia one day as she stood admiring the tree, "in town I don't like chokecherry trees; they drop their fruit on the sidewalk, and I step on it. It messes up my shoes. But out here in the country no fruit seems to fall. Why? Do birds eat it too fast?"

They do indeed. Nearly all birds seem to like chokecherries. So, though the tree tends to form thickets where one doesn't especially desire them, we are glad to have them for the sake of their May beauty and for their fruit for wildlife.

Botanically it is *Prunus virginiana*. Its leaves are not shiny like those of black cherry, and its fruit clusters are more compact; where the fruit joins the stem, no tiny sepals are present as they are in black cherry. Though I have made jelly of both these cherries, we prefer the black as it's sweeter. However, chokecherries mixed with elderberries and flavored with lemon make a delicious spread.

Pin cherry, or bird cherry, *Prunus pennsylvanica*, is another member of this family, this one growing along roadsides or on top of forsaken hills. In May we can see the shiny white clouds of bloom on Pine Ridge when we are a quarter of a mile away. All parts of this slender small tree sparkle;

the bark glistens, the leaves have a luster, the scarlet fruits are like jewels. And pin-cherry jelly fairly shimmers.

Pioneers had a recipe for a cherry liqueur: whole raw cherries and sugar were put into a jar and covered with rum. The jar was closed and set aside for a number of weeks to allow the magic fermentation to take place. The result was called "cherry bounce," and the fruit itself was "rum cherry."

If you want to eat them raw, both cherries and plums must be fully ripe for you to get their full bouquet. An old umbrella can catch the ripe fruit as you shake a limb; only the ripe cherries fall if you shake gently. Those slightly under the peak of ripeness are all right for jelly or juice or cherry and plum butter.

One day Happy led me to the edge of the stream, where a half-dozen marsh marigolds caught the sun and glistened. Above them were puccoons, just beginning to open. I made a mental note to come back and search the puccoons in August for their tiny white seeds. Since I had failed in trying to transplant this most desirable wild flower, I would try planting its seed. I would soak it in warm water for a day or two, as I do the seed of lupine, and then plant it in sandy, sunny places.

When I returned to the yard, Henry was on a ladder in front of his workshop. He held something gray and ragged.

"What are you doing?"

"This robin's nest was in the wires."

I took the nest from him and examined it. "They've used the cloth I put out for them, and here are some strings and some of Trig's hair."

I went into the house and found a worn work shirt of Henry's that I could cut into narrow strips. These I hung over the branches of the red pine near the outhouse. Before nightfall we had to scare the robins away from the wires several times, for they wanted to rebuild there. By morning, however, they had settled for the red pine, and they built low enough for us to peer into the nest and watch the young.

"The upland plover is here," Henry announced at dinner.

That's something to be excited about, for this little bird travels all the way from the Argentine to build his home and raise his young in our marsh. He nests along with the Chinese ring-necked pheasant, but unlike the big bird he gets his babies out of the nest before hay-cutting time rolls round, when so many pheasant nests (eggs or chicks) are destroyed by the mower. The plover's babies are able to run as soon as their down is dry.

"I saw only one," said Henry, "but the grasses were waving close by, so I suspect the young were there too."

I love early morning in May. A fog is nearly always hovering above the meadow. Sometimes it slips in just a half hour after sunset, turning our valley and woods into a Millet painting, misty blue and brown and tan, shadowy and indistinct and lovely. At four-thirty in the morning the fog is dense on the water, leaving only the nearest white oaks visible from my window. At five-thirty it has been pulled away by the rising sun, and the terrace is quivering with wildlife.

One morning last May I counted four gray squirrels, two quail, four whitethroats, two song sparrows, a chipmunk, and four blue jays, all within a few feet of the door. They remained during our breakfast and then went away for a while. Within minutes a dove, a redwing, and a junco arrived, a little field mouse shot across the stones, a small brown bird hopped nervously about in the red pine but never got the courage to join the others, a white-breasted nuthatch clung upside down on the oak to which the hammock was attached, and down the bridge road a brown thrasher kicked up leaves, disdaining our corn and buckwheat.

Chippy returned seven times during one hour and filled each of his cheek pouches with three sunflower seeds; then he ran down his hole by the lupine to store his prize. I think he must be a terrible braggart among the animals, for he doesn't eat what he stores at this time of year. His motive is probably just to be able to boast of his wealth. Perhaps he and Dartmouth, in the Pine Room, have a sociable evening now and then to talk about their stores.

"Look, Mother," observed Virginia, "the blue jays and the squirrels eat only the kernel of the corn. The gray squirrel drops the hull as he bites into it; the jay takes his to a limb and pecks it open with two hard blows."

We stood together, shoulders touching, while we watched. Finally I said, "How about bringing me some apple and cherry blossoms for the gray jug?"

She was back in a little while, carrying also a branch of red pine for the yellow teapot.

"I think the red-pine candles are the prettiest of all just now," she said, "so orange and compact, like a gathered ribbon rosette."

One of Henry's Maytime jobs is the disking of the fire lane. The first disking breaks the sod and the second turns it under. While on his fire-lane job he watches for birds and reports to me on those he has seen. The eastern bluebirds have arrived two months earlier and are followed in early May by the indigo bunting. The migrant blue warblers come a little later.

"These, with the all-year residents, the blue jays and

belted kingfishers, sure make this a blue month, don't they?"
he observed one day.

"Yes, in color, but not in spirit. I guess I never have been
blue in May."

"Nice month," he agreed.

I took a walk downstream in the late afternoon to look
for a bunting. Because of his brilliant color he keeps mostly
to very dense brushy areas, where it is difficult for predators to see him. He builds low and raises his young there,
but when he wants to sing, he goes to the heights. So I
looked for him in the silver and red maples. Soon I heard
his thin little voice coming from high in my favorite maple
near the acre of hepaticas.

Knowing from experience that I'd not be able to find his
nest in May, I didn't look for it. When the leaves of alder,
birch, and willow fall in October, then I find the buntings'
compact cups of grass and strips of cedar bark in crotches
from eighteen inches to four feet off the ground.

On the way back to the house I found the nest of blue
grosbeaks, a rarity in our region since this bird habitually
nests in states farther south, where spring comes earlier. As
I stooped to tie my tennis shoe, I saw a brown-and-blue
mottled bird fly away from the ninebark by which I stood.
Carefully hidden in the bush about three feet from the
ground was a sizable nest, loosely made, and from it swung
a strip of paper with printing on it. Leaning closer, I was
able to make out: *The Daily Sentinel*, Nacogdoches, Tex.
My hometown paper! I chuckled at the thought of that piece
of paper printed in a small Texas town now woven into a
bird nest in central Wisconsin. The grosbeak must have
plucked it out of our incinerator. In the nest lay three
bluish-white eggs.

I walked away and sat beneath a birch to await the return of the mother. Suddenly she was sitting tight on the eggs, but I hadn't seen her arrival. Then I heard near me a weak finchlike warbling. In the top of a cranberry bush sat the beautiful male grosbeak, a purplish-blue bird. Cautious and wary, he saw me and took to cover. I didn't see the birds later in the summer.

By the time I had reached the Wildwood that day my arms ached with the squaw-wood I had gathered. I was glad to lay it down along the paths, to outline them. Squaw-wood is a term the Indians used to denote dead wood the squaws picked up or pulled off trees for firewood. May is the first month of the year that allows me to engage in this chore so flavored with the spirit of early Wisconsin. In April we are too busy getting ready for the new season, and April winds are too sharp to encourage so leisurely a stroll as I yearn to make daily in May.

One of my favorite trees in May is the tamarack. Larch and hackmatack are other names for this tree that was here when the giant glaciers slid across the states. When the glaciers melted, leaving great areas covered with debris, the seeds of the tamarack sprouted wherever there was enough moisture. Now in our spongy bogs the tamarack raises its slender spire and covers itself in May with blue-green needles, soft and feathery, less than an inch long. Though it looks so much like an evergreen tree all summer, the tamarack drops its needles in the fall to form a carpet of smoky gold. Then I gather its small round cones, each about the size of a thumbnail, and use them in winter arrangements.

Sometimes I wonder how deep our tamarack roots had to thrust themselves to find a firm bottom. I have read that long, tough root fibers of this tree may go down twenty feet and that the fibers are like the waxed thread used by shoemakers. Indians used these root strings for sewing birch-bark canoes. Indeed, it was the Indians who named this tree, and I understand from tree experts that it is the only native Wisconsin tree that has retained its Indian name. Botanically it is *Larix laricina.*

By the twenty-fifth of May the farm is at its best spring beauty and the weather has quieted somewhat, though occasionally we have light snow flurries and killing frosts until the first of June. On the pool bank is tall yellow *Iris pseudacorus* above forget-me-nots. Though the forget-me-nots are here and there in blue or pink patches all along the stream, they are at their best on the bank beside the guest cottage. There, with butterwort, columbine, bracken, coral-bells, bluebells, woodland phlox, and harebells, the forget-me-nots are in their glory as a sky-blue ground cover and companion for these taller flowers.

During May the frogs are very loud after sunset. One has such a loud and deep voice that we call him Grandfather Bull. He sits on the pool bank and leads the chorus.

From the first to the middle of May many kinds of ducks come to the swimming pool and to Birch Pond, but only the mallards, redheads, and teals have stayed to nest. Now that wild rice is coming up more abundantly, perhaps others will adopt our site. Sandpipers, cranes, and herons seem to prefer the creek to the still water.

In this, the only real spring month with us, we have a few troubles and annoyances as well as many joys. Sandflies, no-see-ums, mosquitoes, and deer flies assault us every time we go outdoors. After the first few days Henry is immune to the pesky things, but I swell whenever I am stung. So I spray myself and my clothes before leaving the house and take along in a jeans pocket a small can of insecticide. I nearly always wear slacks or jeans and shirts or jackets with long sleeves, and a scarf tied around my hair and covering my ears, for the sandflies like to sting at the hairline. When the day is windy the insects are no bother, and after summer really begins, only the mosquitoes are a major concern. Of course, such stinging inhabitants as wasps, bees, yellow-jackets, and hornets have to be watched for all during the season, but in May they have not yet become very active. We are thankful for the lack of chiggers and poisonous snakes.

Next spring one of my major fields of study will be mushrooms, for our oak woodlands are filled with them in fascinating shapes and colors. Beginning in May and lasting through deer season in November, they spring up in tantalizing fashion—even in the corral and my flower beds.

Trout season opens in May, usually early in the month. We therefore have many meals with brook trout as the *piece de résistance*. A tossed green salad with a good deal of fresh watercress from the Wedde is a must with broiled or fried trout. Cornbread sticks go well, too, particularly if the fish has been rolled in corn meal before frying. If it has been floured instead, blueberry muffins taste better. We like a siesta after such a meal.

Goethe said, "*Was mann weiss, sieht mann*"—"one sees what one knows." Believing this, I made some name stakes to place along my nature trails. That is, Henry made the stakes, three by twenty inches, sharpened on one end. Then I painted them white and printed in black the names of the chief flowers to be looked for in each specific area.

The three trails were connected, but seldom was a visitor so sturdy a hiker that he could do the entire route without coming back to the house for rest periods. Customarily we planned to take one trail before lunch, one in midafternoon, and the last about sunset time. For the sake of convenience I numbered them I, II, and III, but we did not always walk them in that order.

Trail I leads from the corral downhill along Fir Lane, past Birch Pond, the best blackberry bramble, the fringed-gentian area, and one of the bog gardens. It follows the stream to the eastern boundary, where the round-leaf hepatica and rattlesnake orchid bloom among lady and maidenhair fern. If one rakes away the leaves, he is sure to find a ground cover of dark-green partridge berry. If a hiker thinks he would rather return to the house by a more level route than the steep hill indicates at this point, he can wade the stream, or walk across a horizontal trunk of a big basswood tree, or cross more conventionally on a bridge of flat stones. From that point he may walk the edge of the timothy field and enjoy the mountain ash and honeysuckle between it and the stream. This route is excellent for bird-watching.

The second trail begins with the steep climb up Big Ridge to the area of the pasques and prairie smoke, the latter still waving its mauve seed pods like feathers in the May breeze. In July *Tephrosia* blooms there; goat's-rue is the unromantic local name for this lovely flower of apricot and gold. In September I have counted a dozen prairie gentian a little farther along the trail.

Beyond our young pines we walk through a grove of red oak growing from acorns planted by Mr. Wentland some twenty years ago to stop a sand-blow. In May the oak leaves are but half-grown and are still a chartreuse color, except on new sprouts coming up at the edge of the grove; on these the leaves are like rose velvet to both the sight and the touch. I sometimes arrange them in a bowl in lieu of flowers, they are so lovely.

Continuing, we enter the cathedral of pines, and silence

falls upon us. The brown carpet absorbs our footsteps, and the ever-present murmur in the highest boughs gently carries away our voices until our lips are stilled. It is as if we were walking in a real cathedral, admiring the arches overhead and the mosaics all around. Be it May or October, the effect on us is the same.

From the pines the path circles the Dump, where grows our only cactus, prickly pear, and then crosses a field where red clover blossoms hide the lark's nest until we are upon it. Only then does the lark flutter off and perform the broken-wing act to distract us. We swing around a windbreak and along the fire lane, where prairie gay-feather (*Liatris spicata*) inspires exclamations during August, but where in May only the low *Ranunculus* and bird's-foot violets greet us.

As we turn north to go back to the house, we come upon a stretch of tractor road bordered by gnarled Scotch pines that, because of infestation by borers, have assumed unnatural shapes. One grows horizontal, making a bench that will seat three adults. One is like a giant corkscrew, and another grows like a shrub with seven trunks. Artists in our party lift sketchbooks from their jackets to catch on paper the unusual forms. Photographers, too, have fun on this part of the trail.

A few feet to the west of these trees is a hillside of exposed glacial gravel, with small stones up to five inches. Rock hounds love this spot. Hazel Maryan, artist and writer, spent practically a whole day there, finding smooth pebbles that could be glued together to make funny fat figures resembling "found sculpture."

Trail III goes from the farmhouse up Middle Ridge to the white-ash grove and then west to Pine Ridge, where we have planted about eight thousand pines. At the north edge of one plantation is a place barren of trees but in which grow several varieties of mosses and lichens, some blooming in May. It is here that those in the party who want to make terrariums find their prettiest specimens. They fill their shoe boxes, brought along for the purpose, by simply cupping their hands over the desired specimen and lifting. The soil is moist sand, allowing the moss to come away easily.

From the highest point on this trail one gets another magnificent view to the north. In the foreground is the red house, beyond it is the pool, and then come the cream-white buckwheat field, the oak and poplar woodland, the corn and bean fields of the Fenskes, the hill that blocks sight of Richford, and the wide, wide expanse of clear sky. Though the colors change with the season, the features remain, and the scene is one that lifts the heart. Once, in the winter, when Virginia was having friends to bobsled and ski, I went on snowshoes to this point. The scene then was like one of Grandma Moses' paintings, with teen-agers in red and blue and yellow scattered on the hillside, sprawled in the valley, and skating on the pool.

Trail III leads downhill to the meadow, where more than half the items in my long list of native flora were discovered. There, too, among the jack pine and dewberries are boulders six to eight feet in diameter. The hikers rest on these boulders and eat the berries if the time is late August. In May they search for yellow lady's-slippers beneath the alders. In June they enjoy pink meadow phlox and Golden Alexander. In July swamp candles, Culver's root, lighten the whole meadow. In September bottle gentians and many varieties of aster attract both human beings and bees.

# X  *Retrospection*

N O W that enough years have gone by for us to gain perspective on our experiences, I think that one of the best times of every day is that period just before we sleep, when we customarily walk out to the parking area and turn our faces upward to listen to the music of the spheres, as night sounds have been called. On a moonless night surely there are more stars over our ridges than anywhere else in the world! The stillness enters our very souls, giving calm and peace.

In the summer we stay to watch the northern lights streak across from the northeast, and we marvel at the phenomenon. In early spring we stay to count similar streaks of cirrus clouds, sometimes as many as sixteen or seventeen, converging to a point in the northeast.

We walk back to the house then and go to bed. But before we sleep, we exchange notes about small pleasant happenings of the day, usually about birds and animals we have seen.

It may be that Henry, while fishing, had a woodchuck visitor in a new area; the animal sat up on his haunches and looked him over and then ambled on without anxiety. Or perhaps I had heard a beautiful song that I had not at first been able to identify, only to find it came from a blue jay! Accustomed as we are to his hawklike screams and crowlike caws, it is really amazing to hear him caroling and twittering as sweetly as a tanager.

I ask Henry why he was especially exhilarated at having a creel full of big browns that day.

"Well, it wasn't the fish," he says, and there's a smile in his voice. "It was something that happened on the Chaffee just above the Delavan shack. I was wading upstream slowly, approaching a bend where I usually raise a good one, when I became aware of something unusual. I saw nothing but felt I was being watched. I searched the right bank with my eyes, and there in the red dogwood and tall grass I saw two large dark eyes staring back at me. It was a doe. And just beyond her head lay a newly dropped fawn, asleep, both within easy reach of my rod tip!"

"Oh, how wonderful!" I exclaim softly.

"I hardly breathed for fear of frightening her, but I kept on wading, one slow step after another, until I rounded the bend and was out of sight. I didn't make a cast there; the swish of my rod might have scared her, but I didn't feel the loser in passing up the chance to raise a big one."

I may tell him I saw the wood lily today. This lily is very special with us. Ever since the day that Alden and Kay White found it and told us where, we have enjoyed its red beauty and have searched in vain for some young ones near. Why is it so alone? High on a hill near the pasques and prairie smoke (*Geum triflorum*) and ruff gentian, it is off to one side of the crest in the shade of a black oak, a solitary lily for at least six years. Why?

Perhaps we mention again the apparent preferences among insects and birds for certain colors among the flowers: bees like the blue ones, moths like the white ones, hummingbirds the red ones, and goldfinches the yellow.

Or maybe we speak of the probability of our getting geese on our small water surfaces. I recall the October day on Liberty Hill, two miles south of us, where Fritz Sheley and his mother stood with me to watch a flock of geese. They were descending rapidly, a ragged ribbon in the north-south flyway.

"Stay perfectly still," I cautioned. "They're Canada 'honkers'; maybe they'll come close to us."

The leader did swing about and head for the gray granite ledge on which we stood. They flew in low over our heads, honking loudly and resonantly, and settled below us in a harvested cornfield near Wood Lake to feast on waste grain.

"It was a thrill," I tell Henry. "They're such wild, magnificent creatures! Their wings are so wide we could feel the breeze they created as they swept by."

"Their wingspread is nearly six feet," says Henry. "We may get some here, though our watering places are smaller than they usually choose except for a temporary resting place."

"Even that would be fine. Our standing corn might attract them. I wish they knew how much I want them."

I may tell him the mallard hen is again bringing her brood to the swimming pool to spend the night. Each season we watch the hour-after-sunset parade. One by one the ducklings slide down the steep bank and plop into the water to swim off behind their mother to a tussock of grass at the far end of the pool. There the mother flattens an area between a boulder and the water and gathers her ducklings beneath her for the night. I watch from the kitchen window. As they swim the length of the pool, which at that hour is reflecting the sunset clouds, they look like gold figurines on a rose and blue mirror.

"It is a scene from Corot," I say, "misty, watery, trees feathery soft, some red and green and blue, graceful, subtle, not much detail . . ."

Just before we sleep is the time also for talking of Virginia. In the early years our conversation was likely to go like this:

"She's maturing rapidly, isn't she? Her choices are wiser now; she thinks of the consequences before deciding."

Then Henry would tease by reminding me that was to be expected since she was *his* daughter, and in his voice there was a vibrancy of love and pride.

But suddenly she *was* mature, a Phi Beta Kappa graduating from the University of Wisconsin with a degree in zoology and French and engaged to be married to one of the young men she had brought to Triple Ridge for weekends with us. Our conversation underwent a change of tone, with much expectation and anticipation. She married Ted Weis, *Doctor* Ted now, for he earned his M.D. at the University of Chicago. While he was serving his internship at Billings Hospital and his residency at Michael Reese Hospital, Virginia mothered their daughter and son and a menagerie of exotic birds, fishes, and animals.

Our conversation nowadays concerns the whole family, and our best times are when six-year-old Erica Lynne and three-year-old Justin Morris come to the farm in the summertime. Erica likes to sit with me in the Pine Room while I read to her, and to make playhouses on the pine-needle carpet, or to ride on top of Grandpater's trailer when it is filled with oak leaves, and often she sketches "like Mommie." Virginia carries her sketch pad with her on every stroll along the paths she used to ride with Trig, and she always visits old Trig, who at twenty-four years of age is still able to do his rocking-horse canter with a stylish air. His owner is Richard Chilewski, to whom she gave the horse in 1958 when she realized she would not have time thereafter to care for him and to ride him regularly. Richard, now a progressive farmer, handles Trig gently and keeps him clean and well fed. Lucky Trig.

Little Justy is fascinated by the hundreds of tadpoles and leopard frogs at Birch Pond, and by Grandpater's tractor, by the red leaves that drift down to caress him in late summer and early fall, and by the many trees that have low limbs for climbing.

Ted enjoys most the opportunity to sleep late in the quiet guest cottage and to lie in my hammock and read his medical journals, to eat trout and watercress fresh from the stream and asparagus only a few minutes from the garden.

He and Henry discuss the future of the pines, and we are happy to know that our "children" love the farm and will care for it after we are gone.

Sometimes we talk of the other young people who helped us get started with all the conservation projects. Howard Fravel still helps us occasionally, for he is now an odd-jobs contractor in Coloma. His two daughters and little son are beautiful children, whom he brings to play among the pines he helped plant a dozen years ago.

Bryan Davis has a degree in law from the University of Texas and is established as an attorney in his and my hometown, Nacogdoches, Texas. Bryan has a son, but Fritz Sheley has three! Fritz received his Ph.D. in Chemistry at the University of Ohio, married a concert pianist, Marie Du Pont, from southern Louisiana, and is now with a large commercial firm in the East. Deep in his heart, however, is his dream of eventually becoming a professor, for he feels about teaching as we do, that it is the *top* profession.

Ray White married a German girl while he was in Germany at the University of Hamburg pursuing graduate work in limnology. When he returns to Wisconsin this year he will receive his Ph.D. in zoology.

The Fenske boys returned to Richford after their military service and bought farms adjoining and near their parents' farms. They are a family concern now known as Fenske Farms, Inc. Howard works part-time with the Conservation Department in the winter and in the summer helps run a "pickle" weighing station the father and sons built in Richford near Wichner's Store. Harold is trying to slow down now, leaving most of the chores and hard work to his able sons. Darrell is a giant of a man, all farmer, but he takes the time to enjoy wildlife on the farms, and he still keeps a watchful eye on our place. We expect his and Howard's children to come often to Triple Ridge.

Gretchen Ihde and Jeanne Larson, the two Madison girls who helped us paint and plant, are leading interesting lives. Jeanne married Tom Houle, who is with the Regional Planning Commission of Lake County, Ill. Jeanne has two sons and has continued her singing in civic choruses and church choirs. Gretchen married Hal Serri, assistant professor of anthropology at Beloit College. They spent a year in Oaxaca, Mexico and another in Syria, and they have a son. Gretchen has continued her affiliation with the Madison Civic Symphony and Sinfonia, playing first violin.

Some day we'll have a reunion of Jeanne's, Gretchen's, and Virginia's families and what fun it will be. Virginia will play the classical guitar and Gretch the violin, while Ted, Jeanne, and Virginia will sing ballads. Tom and Hal will pose for Virginia to sketch them, and all will reminisce about the way they helped Ruth and Henry Pochmann get off to a good start at work none of us knew anything about.

Our reality was once only a dream, the kind of dream many of the world's peoples have dreamed. Because we live in the United States we had the freedom to try making that dream come true. Because we live in the wide Midwest we had a choice of land. Because we live in Wisconsin, the home of the late Aldo Leopold, father of conservation as it is known today, we were able to absorb knowledge in quantity and quality that few other states offer.

Triple Ridge has become a place for relaxation, where beauty lies so warm about us that we feel uplifted and peaceful, happy and good. Our serious intention—to renew the soil and water and forests and to re-create the right environment for wildlife—has been, and still is, a challenge.

But I have found another kind of renewal, that of my inner resources. I can measure myself against the pines and ever-flowing springs; I can see myself in close relation with other living things, a part of the natural world. I gain spiritually as I observe life and death and resurrection, and I grow in my capacity to feel and think as I experience the poignancy and poetry of the Wild. This place—our place—has given me strength and energy and new enthusiasm for this world we live in, rewards that I hope will be inherited by my descendants.

# A Note About The Author

RUTH FOUTS POCHMANN was born in Nacogdoches, Texas in 1903. She received her B.A. from Stephen F. Austin State University after three years of undergraduate work at Southern Methodist University, and her M.A. in English and American Literature from Columbia University. She married Henry A. Pochmann, a university professor, in 1928, and together they have traveled extensively in Europe and America. Mrs. Pochmann, who now resides in Madison, Wisconsin with her husband, was named "Woman of the Year in Conservation" by the Wisconsin Federation of Woman's Clubs in 1966 and has served as Conservation Chairman and Landscape Design Chairman for Wisconsin garden clubs and for the Madison District. She is a prolific writer and her short stories, poems and articles have been published in numerous magazines, journals and newspapers. She has also written a genealogy entitled *Some Early Texas Families*.

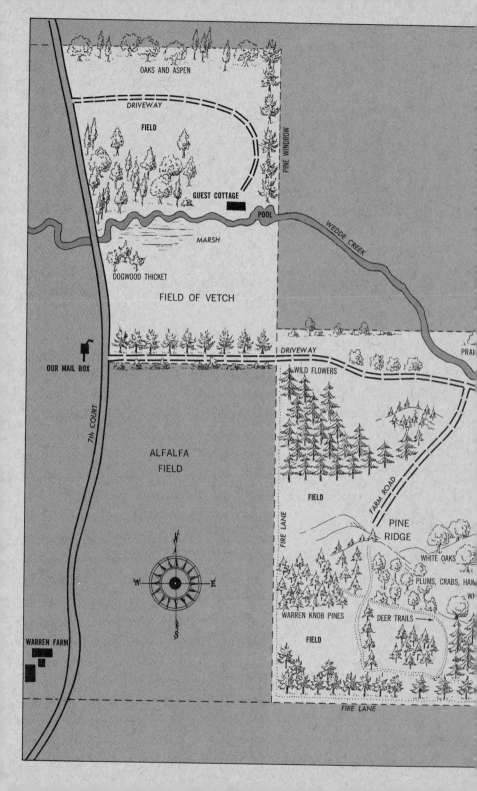